MW01502970

The Practice of Contentment

How to Acquire Natural Wealth

*For Tammy,
with great
appreciation for the
quality person you are.
Oliver*

Oliver Ross, J.D., Ph.D.

Joss Publications
Scottsdale, Arizona

The Practice of Contentment: How to acquire natural wealth

Copyright © 2015 by Oliver Ross

The content of this book is for general instruction only and is for use at your own risk. It is not intended to replace a one-on-one relationship with a qualified professional nor is it intended as a substitute for advice provided by a qualified health provider. The author is not rendering medical, health, psychological, or any other kind of personal professional services in this book. Rather, it is intended for general education, inspiration and information only, to help you make informed decisions about your wellbeing and habits. Each person's physical, emotional, and spiritual condition is unique. The instructions in this book are based on the author's education and personal experiences and are not intended to replace or interrupt the reader's relationship with a physician, mental health professional or other provider.

All information is intended to be as accurate and up-to-date as possible, but typographical and content mistakes may occur. Due to the dynamic nature of the Internet, any links or websites contained in this book may have changed since publication.

To contact the author, visit
www.practicecontentment.com

Printed in the United States of America
First Edition published by Joss Publications LLC, 8350 East Raintree Drive, Suite 205, Scottsdale, Arizona 85260

ISBN-10: 0692554335
EAN-13: 9780692554333

For my wife, Jocelyn,
for whom
my appreciation
and love have no limits.

Contents

INTRODUCTION

"Contentment is natural wealth."
Socrates[1]

In today's world, discontent seems to be the prevailing mood. Despite the fact that most of us have plenty of resources, far greater than those required to meet our essential needs for food, shelter and social contact, we are still mostly dissatisfied, disgruntled, depressed or similarly discontent.

Why is it that most of us feel such discontentment? How does our dissatisfaction affect our emotions, behavior, relationships, and health? And, what can we do to be content?

The answers to these questions first came into focus when I began to pay attention to what was really going on inside me. I noticed that each time I felt down or otherwise discontented and took the time to examine these feelings, I could mentally trace their origin back to a thought I had just experienced. I became aware that, in one way or another and regardless of the circumstances, these thoughts always related to wanting more, better or different of someone or something: *more* affection,

---

[1] The ancient Greek philosopher who established the "Socratic method," a form of inquiry and discussion which laid the groundwork for Western systems of logic and philosophy.

money, and so on; *better* health, friends, and so forth; *different* parents, social life, and the like; and on and on. No matter what the particulars, I noticed that all of these thoughts invariably related to getting or achieving more, better or different circumstances.

The answers to these questions came into even sharper focus when I noticed that, no matter how slight or great, my discontent was always rooted in the fundamentally mistaken belief that getting or achieving more of this, better of that, or a different kind of something or someone would make me feel content. I realized that beyond my essential needs, no amount of anything—from possessions, to recognition, to affection, to accomplishments—had ever made me content. They may have made me happy, at least temporarily, but these circumstances never gave me the peace of mind and sense of satisfaction characteristic of contentment.

As I gained this heightened clarity, I began to earnestly examine my thoughts. I wanted to understand why I continuously bought into the mistaken belief that more, better or different of someone or something would make me feel content. I sought to comprehend why I would time and again forget about the inherent falsity of these thoughts and, thus, consistently cause myself varying degrees of discontent.

That was also when I began to develop the habit of paying particular attention to any degree of discontent I felt. Instead of ignoring, suppressing or avoiding these feelings, I would deliberately pause to ferret out the more, better or different thought that preceded them.

It was in this way that I eventually discovered that all of the more, better or different thoughts behind my discontent were *unappreciative* in nature. Without fail these thoughts were based in a lack of appreciation for the things I already possessed or achieved.

It was also in this way that I discovered that a lot of other people seemed predominately predisposed to the mistaken belief that they don't have enough as well. Like me, their thoughts were largely centered on what they didn't have rather than what they did.

This book is about what I have discovered regarding discontentment in relation to more, better and different thinking—which I will hereafter sometimes refer to as "unappreciative more, better, different," "not-enough" and "unappreciative" thinking or thoughts. Based on the premise that we all have the inborn capacity to create the serenity and satisfaction that comprises contentment, this book is also about how to transform the internal energy generated by this type of thinking into a catalyzer of contentment instead of discontentment.

It is important to note, however, that this book is in no way intended to suggest that all of our more, better and different thinking is inherently bad, wrong, or mistaken, because this is definitely not the case. As I will later explain in detail, not-enough thinking is a natural product of the way our brains are structured and how we have been conditioned to think. It is not good nor bad, right nor wrong; it is simply an integral part of our humanness.

Nor is this book intended to suggest that it is possible or even desirable to entirely eliminate the occurrence of unappreciative more, better, different thinking. Quite the opposite; it is meant to provide the information needed to minimize the negative emotional and behavioral consequences of this type of thinking and thereby generate increasingly frequent moments of contentment.

It follows, therefore, that the practice of contentment is not an all-or-nothing proposition. It's perfectly okay to think about and pursue more, better or different things. It's part of being human to do so and has motivated many wonderfully life-enhancing advances in medicine, science and technology. Instead, it is the extent to which our minds are filled with unappreciative versus appreciative thoughts that is of penultimate importance in determining whether or not we will be discontent versus content, not the formation of one or more of any kind of not-enough thoughts. Whether rich or poor in material things and/or individual achievements, contentment comes during those moments when our mind is predominately populated with the energy of thoughts that are appreciative in nature.

This book is divided into three major parts. The first part is about "Awareness." To start, I will discuss the importance of becoming knowledgeable about the different aspects of more, better, different thinking as well as the origins, nature and negative emotional and behavioral consequences of such thought patterns.

The second part is devoted to "Acceptance." In this part I will delineate and describe the different components of acceptance: acknowledgment, surrender, and forgiveness. I will also explain how acceptance mixed with awareness neutralizes the negative energy generated by our not-enough thoughts and clears the way for the formation of internal energy fields which are devoid of unappreciative more, better, different thoughts and thus receptive to the infusion of appreciative ones.

Finally, in the third part, "Action," I will recount various ways I have found facilitative in furthering the development of a predominately appreciative state of mind. These assorted actions have helped me enrich and prolong the contentment derived from becoming aware and accepting of the advent of a not-enough thought.

Each chapter within the three parts of this book also includes my "Reflections." These are my personal experiences and insights pertaining to the subject matter, which I hope will not only provide additional knowledge about practicing contentment but also give rise to reflections and understandings about similar experiences in your own life.

My observation is that becoming proficient in the practice of contentment takes time and effort. Our thoughts continually come and go, often without any apparent rhyme or reason, and it takes a good deal of patience and persistence to stay alert to the occurrence of our not-enough ones. After all, the prevailing mood of discontent that most of us feel didn't come about overnight; so it would be unrealistic to expect that it will suddenly change. This is why practicing contentment is an art. It is also why practitioners are encouraged to aspire for progress not perfection. Nonetheless, unlike many religious and contemplative practices which can take months and even years to develop, practitioners of contentment can realistically expect relatively quick results.

Clearly, the art of practicing contentment presents both challenge and opportunity. As a practitioner, you will undoubtedly be confronted by seemingly endless varieties of not-enough thoughts. At the same time, however, these challenges will most certainly provide you with countless opportunities to hone your skills in cultivating the natural wealth of contentment.

Part One
AWARENESS

"Let us not look back in anger,
or forward in fear, but around in awareness."
James Thurber[2]

---

[2] A celebrated 20th Century American author, journalist, playwright, and cartoonist.

Chapter 1

The Importance of Awareness

"The ultimate value of life depends upon awareness."
Aristotle[3]

In general terms, awareness means being knowledgeable about something. As humans, we have a unique capacity for introspection which allows us to become self-aware. In the practice of contentment, awareness allows a practitioner to become knowledgeable about the inner workings of his or her mind by cultivating the introspection that brings forth self-awareness. Like a flashlight illuminates darkness, awareness illuminates the occurrence of unappreciative more, better, different thinking.

It was the British statesman and philosopher Francis Bacon who said that "knowledge is power." When practicing contentment, becoming knowledgeable about our not-enough thoughts provides us with the power to be able to choose

---

[3] The ancient Greek philosopher and scientist who created the scientific method of investigation.

how and to what extent these types of thoughts adversely affect our feelings and behaviors. Without the illumination provided by awareness, we would remain in the dark about these types of thoughts and how they negatively impact us. However, with the illumination provided by awareness, we can comprehend the whys and wherefores of these types of thoughts and understand how to deal with them in contentment-cultivating ways.

Therefore as a practitioner of contentment, it is crucial that you steadfastly cultivate awareness of the initiation of not-enough thinking. This insight is the single most essential requirement for avoiding the negative consequences which otherwise inevitably follow this type of thinking. With a willingness to commit to becoming aware of the occurrence of your not-enough thoughts, you can begin to recognize the voice in your head that would have you mistakenly believe that a surplus of more, better or different of something or someone will make you content. Indeed, with awareness you will possess the internal wherewithal to follow the prescription given by the late positive thinking advocate Dr. Norman Vincent Peale: "Change your thoughts, and change your world." Each time you become aware of a not-enough thought, you will have knowledge to transform its internal energy into a catalyst for contentment rather than a disseminator of discontentment—and thereby "change your world."

Reflections

When I look back on my life in the years before becoming aware of my not-enough thoughts, I'm amazed at how little I knew about my thoughts in general much less my not-enough ones. It's not simply that I didn't know about these unappreciative thoughts; it's that *I didn't know that I didn't know* about them, an impenetrable double-blind of darkness that made it impossible for any light of awareness to shine through.

This is not to say that before becoming aware of these types of thoughts I didn't know anything about the inner workings of my mind—because I did. In fact for decades before this realization, I was intermittently involved in individual and group psychotherapy, several self-help programs and self-actualization groups, and different religious activities and spiritual practices. I had even earned advanced degrees in clinical and behavioral psychology. Yet despite all of these experiences, I didn't realize that my discontent was a direct result of my own internal not-enough thinking, instead of some external circumstance.

However, I am now acutely aware of and profoundly grateful for the many ways in which each and every one of these involvements contributed to the knowledge and experience required for me to truly understand the importance of becoming aware of my not-enough thoughts. For it is with this awareness that I have truly changed my world.

Chapter 2

Contentment and Discontentment

*"When you are discontent, you always want more,
more, more. Your desire can never be satisfied.
But when you practice contentment,
you can say to yourself, 'Oh yes - I already
have everything that I really need.'"*
The Dalai Lama[4]

Each and every feeling we experience, including contentment and discontentment, is a bodily reaction to the thoughts produced by our minds. As such, any and all of our feelings are directly linked to our thoughts, with the nature of our thoughts shaping how we feel.

Contentment is the way in which your body reacts when your thoughts are mostly *appreciative* in nature; i.e., when your thinking is predominately imbued with appreciation for your present-moment circumstances, regardless of whether you consider them good, bad or indifferent. When you feel content, it signifies that you are grateful for who you are and what you have in the here and now, regardless of what happened or didn't happen in the past and what may or may not

---

[4] The 14th Dalai Lama, Tenzin Gyatso, who is the spiritual and temporal leader of Tibetan people and a Noble Peace Prize recipient.

happen in the future. This is why one person may be content with having just enough material possessions to meet his or her essential needs, while another person may be deeply discontent despite having a sizeable surplus of these things. This concept is illustrated by the fact that, after a brief period of elation, two-thirds of lottery winners sink into even greater discontent than before "winning".

It isn't the number of possessions, achievements and other things that a person has accumulated or attained that determines whether or not he or she is content. Instead, what matters most for contentment is whether a person's state of mind is mostly appreciative as opposed to unappreciative in nature. This is what Socrates understood when he defined contentment as "natural wealth." He recognized the emotional wealth that accrues when our mindsets are mostly appreciative of what we have and who we are. Benjamin Franklin also understood this when he defined discontentment as "the feeling that makes rich men poor." He understood that when our state of mind is mostly unappreciative, we rob ourselves of the natural wealth of contentment.

There are, of course, different levels of contentment and discontentment. While contentment can range from slight satisfaction to sustained serenity, discontentment can vary from mild annoyance to intense anger. Further, there is also a clear causal connection between our thoughts and feelings, with our level of contentment fluctuating in relation to whether our thoughts are largely appreciative versus unappreciative at any given moment.

How can someone remain content despite, for example, having recently experienced financial problems, currently suffering from ill health, and understanding that her future is bound to include difficulties?

The answer is that, regardless of everything that has been, presently is, or might be in the future, the thoughts produced by this person's mind are predominately appreciative in nature, allowing her to experience contentment in spite of her external circumstances. In other words, this person's mind is largely free of disturbance by memories of her past financial problems, grievances about her ill health, and worries about future difficulties so that at the present moment she has cultivated a good measure of natural wealth.

It also shows that the thoughts produced by this person's mind are grounded in the realities of her present-moment circumstances and, as such, are trustworthy. Because this person's thoughts are undisturbed by subjective memories of the past, complaints about current circumstances, and worries about the future, she can trust the accuracy of her emotions. In other words, she can trust that her gut is accurately assessing the reality of the situation at hand, as well as what actions are likely to be helpful versus harmful to create contentment.

On the other hand, what does it say about a person's state of mind if he feels despondent, depressed, or otherwise discontent as a result of his past, present, or possible future circumstances?

The answer is that it shows that the thoughts produced by his mind are predominately unappreciative in nature; i.e., that they mostly consist of troubling memories of the past, grievances about the present, or worries about the future. It signifies that his mind is mired in dislike or perhaps even disdain for what was, presently is, or may come to pass.

It also demonstrates that this person's thoughts are based in his own particular perceptions of the past or speculations about the future. These thoughts reflect his personal points of view and, as such, are untrustworthy. After all, our interpretations of the interactions we have had with others as well as the ways in which various situations and events occurred are highly subjective, as are our imaginings about future experiences. Furthermore, these interpretations and imaginings are apt to change over time, making them representative of our individual "truth" at one moment but not necessarily another.

Finally, we can observe that this type of mindset will continue to cause unpleasant emotions that contribute to this person's discontentment. In other words, his very own thoughts will continue to rob him of the natural wealth of contentment.

Reflections

I imagine that many of you can look back on your life and recognize one particular event or perhaps even several that profoundly changed its direction. For me, this change of direction came about as a result of what some people would describe as a "breakdown." Instead I call this life-altering experience a "breakout."

Before this breakout, my mind was so rampant with not-enough thoughts that I was persistently plagued with varying degrees of anxiety, worry and fear. I tried to cope with this overwhelm by working almost 24/7, first while practicing law and building my law firm and then as general manager of my parents' company while also a nighttime student in an organizational psychology Master's degree program. Amidst this busyness, I was also taking valium and smoking marijuana. After all, having totally bought into the belief that "the harder you work the luckier you get," my thoughts were predominately focused on being "luckier" than everyone else in accomplishing and acquiring more, better and different things. Indeed, at that time the very idea of appreciating the things I had already achieved or acquired was completely foreign to me; way off my radar screen. Sure, some of my thoughts were appreciative in nature, for instance, those about my wife and children; however, truth be told, they were far less frequent and impactful than my not-enough ones.

And so it was that before this breakout I was completely unaware of the great extent to which my unappreciative thinking was damaging my effectiveness, relationships and health. In fact, although I can laugh about it now, back then I used to tell people that my goal in life was to "use it up." I wanted to use up every bit of energy I had to get and accomplish the more, better and different things that were at that time of quintessential importance to me: the success and acclaim that, regardless of the cost to me and my family, I mistakenly believed would prove to one and all, especially my parents, that I was intelligent and accomplished enough to deserve their admiration and perhaps even love. So, like a hamster on a running-wheel, I relentlessly ran after more, better and different accomplishments only to unwittingly cause myself increasingly greater discontent and damage. Therefore, it is not surprising that before this breakout so many of my emotions were untrustworthy and thus produced behaviors that were less than helpful and frequently harmful.

But in late 1991 a series of totally unexpected and traumatic circumstances coalesced, culminating in my "breakout." By mid-1991, I had been running my parents' company for about four years. In this position, I was in charge of all management decisions and nearly doubled gross sales and profits. I had also completed most of my course work for a Master's degree in organizational psychology, focusing on "Workaholism" as the subject of my Master's thesis. After all, I was very proud of and even boastful about my willingness to work harder and longer than anyone else.

However, later in 1991 I happened upon a book about workaholism entitled "*Working Ourselves to*

Death" by Diane Fassel, PhD. When I found out that she was offering a three-day workshop about workaholism in Boulder, Montana, I enrolled. I thought that attending this workshop would be a great experience to include in my Master's thesis, although I marvel that I actually went because for several years prior I had been suffering increasingly greater anxiety and nighttime panic attacks, was afraid to sleep alone, and, just two days before leaving, was shocked to my core when out of the blue my father angrily demanded that I defer all subsequent business decisions to him (which I later found out was instigated by my mother's baseless fear that I was scheming to push her out of the company).

I arrived at the workshop during the afternoon of Friday, November 1, 1991 and learned that there would be a group meeting that evening as well as several 12-Steps meetings the next morning. These included both Alcoholic Anonymous and Workaholics Anonymous meetings. I believed that this was an educational workshop, so I was somewhat surprised to see these 12-Steps meetings on the schedule. Since I had never had a drinking problem and was still in complete denial about my workaholism, I reckoned that I would just skip them.

There were about thirty people in the group meeting that first evening, including Diane Fassel who asked each of us to share our "story" as it related to workaholism. Never one to shy away from speaking up, I was the first to volunteer. I boasted to everyone that I only required three or four hours of sleep each night, had built my law firm to over forty lawyers and one hundred staff, had almost doubled the size and income of my parents' company in the last four years, and so on, only mentioning as an aside my panic attacks and use of valium and marijuana.

I still remember the utter silence that filled the room when I finished my story. And I will never forget when Diane broke this silence by looking me in the eye and saying, "I am terrified for you, Oliver. You are in the final stages of your disease. I suggest that you seriously consider immediate in-patient treatment!"

My first thought was "*what disease? I don't have a disease.*" But then, I felt my anxiety beginning to mount and within seconds found myself on the floor sobbing hysterically. To say the least, I had lost all control of my emotions, could not stop crying, and was scared to death.

The next few hours were surreal. The rest of the group seemed to take my distress in stride, as most of them had worked with Diane before and were familiar with such crises. After continuing to cry uncontrollably for what felt like hours, someone helped me move to the other side of the room. There, several mattresses had been placed for what I later learned was called "deep processing," a method Diane had developed to help people get in touch with the childhood and other traumatic experiences which were causing their addictions to a substance or a behavior. It was then, as I lay on a mattress enveloped in extreme mental and emotional pain, that I suddenly experienced a profound awakening. It was truly what I would describe as a spiritual awakening. Images appeared of a deceased Rabbi whom I had looked up to in my youth as a paragon of virtue. Prayers spontaneously surfaced that I hadn't thought about, much less voiced, for decades. A crystal clear awareness arose in which I was able to see how a serendipitous series of coincidences had culminated with my studying of psychology, writing a thesis about workaholism, and, in turn, attending this workshop—all to afford me the opportunity to change my thoughts and change my world such that I did not reach the final stage of my disease: self-destruction and perhaps even death.

This awakening was the beginning, but certainly not the end, of my breakout. Throughout the rest of the weekend, it took my best efforts to barely stay afloat in wave after wave of excruciating emotions which intermittently washed over and incapacitated me. This transformation did not stop there. From Montana, I flew to Phoenix, Arizona to meet my wife for a few days. I had planned to attend a business meeting along with spending time with my wife (my usual "working vacation" modus operandi). But my emotions were so unstable that I hardly slept that night and decided to cancel the meeting. Instead, I chose to drive to the treatment center in Tucson, Arizona that Diane Fassel had recommended. Like my law firm disintegrating, my studying of psychology, my choosing workaholism as the subject matter of my Master's thesis, and my being verbally assaulted by my father, this was definitely another "coincidence"— God's way of guiding while remaining anonymous. Although my wife and I lived in California, there we were in Arizona where the opportunity for treatment existed.

Once again I marvel at my having been graced with the capacity to cancel my business meeting, rent a car, and drive to the treatment center in Tucson. In fact, I told my wife that, although I had called to arrange for a tour of the center, I had no intention whatsoever of staying. But then, while my wife and I were halfway through the tour, yet another wave of emotion washed over and incapacitated me. This was when, despite my deep trepidation, I somehow had the sense to submit to twenty-eight days of in-patient treatment—which turned out to consist of recovery-related activities including daily individual and group psychotherapy, and Workaholics Anonymous and other 12-Steps meetings.

Those twenty-eight days of treatment were extremely difficult for me to say the least. For the first week or so, waves of anxiety, fear and other debilitating emotions kept drowning me no matter how hard I tried to stay afloat. The uncontrollable crying these emotions evoked lessened in the following weeks but never completely subsided. The entire time I felt lonely and disoriented, with everyone and everything seeming foreign to me. Yet, despite it all, deep down I somehow knew that I was on the right path.

Within a few days of returning home from treatment, I resigned from my parents' company. Without going into detail about what transpired between us in those few days, it will suffice to say that my parents never forgave me for "betraying and embarrassing them" by undergoing treatment. Looking back, I can understand their reaction, but I can also see how this was yet another time in which I was graced with the deep internal knowing that I had to fundamentally change my life; that it was literally a matter of life and death for me to resign from my parents' company and do everything else I could to learn new ways of living my life.

And so for the next few years my wife and I used our savings to support our family, while I concentrated on my recovery from workaholism, earned a Master's degree in clinical psychology, and, in 1994, received a doctorate degree in behavioral psychology with an emphasis on addictions. Obviously, my breakout and treatment were nothing short of life-changing for me. Indeed, they were life-saving. I am absolutely certain that without my breakout I would have long before now literally worked myself to death!

Chapter 3

Contentment and Happiness

"Contentment brings supreme happiness."
Yoga Sutra 2.42[5]

Contentment and happiness are closely related. They both feel good and are commonly considered positive (i.e., pleasurable) emotions. Indeed, most of us regard contentment and happiness as being so similar that their meanings have become interchangeable if not synonymous. Yet these two emotions actually differ in several significant ways.

First, the thoughts which generate contentment are markedly different in nature than those which generate happiness. Whereas contentment derives from a thought that is *appreciative* in nature, happiness stems from a thought that is *expectant* in nature. For example, thoughts that are expectant in nature include our expectations of ourselves (for instance, to be successful), our expectations of others (say, our spouse), and our expectations of how a situation or event will transpire (for example, the outcome of a disagreement). When our expectations are fulfilled, we are likely to feel pleased, good, glad or

---

[5] Yoga "sutras" are a list of ancient Indian Hindu aphorisms.

likewise happy; but when what we anticipate doesn't happen, we are apt to feel mad, bad, sad, or similarly unhappy.

Another reason why contentment and happiness are markedly different is that appreciative thoughts typically generate an overall sense of satisfaction and serenity, like the soothing sensation of taking a warm bath. On the other hand, thoughts that are expectant in nature typically generate a sense of excitement and exhilaration, like the rush of riding the crest of a wave.

Finally, while both happiness and contentment are inside jobs, they are quite different in terms of prerequisite conditions. Whereas happiness is dependent on countless uncontrollable external circumstances coming together, contentment is solely dependent on our internal state of mind being predominately appreciative.

It's plausible, therefore, that what we commonly experience as happiness is actually just a decrease in the degree of discontent we feel. In other words, sensations of happiness may actually arise when certain external conditions coalesce in a fashion that fulfills one of our expectations and therefore lessens our discontent. The late renowned essayist and short story writer Joseph Epstein expressed this concept when he stated in *The Wall Street Journal*, "The good life has a great deal to do with contentment and satisfaction—and nothing whatsoever to do with the fool's gold called happiness." He seems to have understood that, while it's pleasurable to feel happy and most of us have many different ways and means by which to feel that way, happiness pales in emotional value when compared to contentment, just as the brassy luster of pyrite (aka "fool's gold") is without economic value when compared to that of real gold.

Reflections

I first became aware of the implications of expectant thoughts about five years after my breakout when I read Neale Donald Walsch's book, *Conversations with God: An Uncommon Dialogue (Book 2)*. In this book Walsch quotes "God" as saying, "Expectation is the greatest source of unhappiness." Before coming across this passage, it had never occurred to me that there was a connection between my expectations and my happiness. As I had previously failed to appreciate the connection between not-enough thinking and discontent, before reading this quote I was totally in the dark about the origins, nature and consequences of unhappiness. But, thankfully, I was so deeply moved by this quote that I began to investigate the whys and wherefores of expectant thoughts in general and mine in particular.

I discovered that the varying degrees of unhappiness generated by my unfulfilled expectant thoughts were based in my erroneous expectation that I could *control* other people and the outcomes of situations and events. In actuality, the most I could do is *influence* what anyone else does, says or thinks, or the outcome of any particular situation or event. I came to understand that it is delusional for me (or anyone else) to expect otherwise. I also discovered that the deep-seated anger I periodically felt, for instance towards my parents, was really just a hostile form of self-pity. The only way to rid myself of this self-pity was to take responsibility for my expectant thoughts. In other words, I finally understood that my resentments had nothing whatsoever to do with my parents or anyone else but everything to do with my very own unmet expectant thoughts.

So, considering this connection between expectations and happiness, does this mean that having expectant thoughts and feeling excited or exhilarated when an expectation comes to pass is a bad thing? Or, does it mean that a practitioner of contentment should seek to eradicate any type of expectant thought and reject any happiness he or she feels as a result of it being fulfilled?

Of course not! Expectations are just thoughts. Like our unappreciative more, better, different thoughts, and for that matter any others, it's counterproductive to judge them as good or bad, right or wrong, or moral or immoral. They are simply part of being human. Instead of trying to eradicate them or reject the happiness which these thoughts may generate, practitioners of contentment need only strive to remain aware of their occurrence. With this awareness, you can recognize that any measure of happiness you experience from an expectation being fulfilled is of little or no value when compared to the natural wealth generated by your appreciative thoughts. Like fool's gold compared to real gold, your expectant thoughts may appear exciting or exhilarating yet fail to offer the genuine emotional value gained from appreciation.

Chapter 4

The Willingness Factor

"Nothing is easy to the unwilling."
Thomas Fuller[6]

Willingness is the readiness to do something we value. Like yeast gives rise to bread, in the context of the practice of contentment, willingness is the internal energy that gives rise to our conscious commitment to strive to become aware of and accept the occurrence of not-enough thinking.

It is willingness that generates the internal energy required to become aware of the whys and wherefores of not-enough thinking. It is also willingness that generates the internal energy needed to become knowledgeable about the contentment-cultivating processes and actions described in Parts Two and Three.

Willingness, then, is the predisposition to move forward in garnering the natural wealth that accrues from waking up to the reality that an excess of more, better and different things can never make us content—regardless of how much

---

[6] A 17th Century prolific author, noted historian and Anglican churchman.

we acquire or accomplish. It is the internal fuel that fires the practice of contentment.

For these reasons, there is great truth in the adage, "Where there is a will, there is a way." With willingness we have the internal energy needed to free ourselves from endlessly suffering the contentment-constricting consequences of our not-enough thoughts. With willingness we are also ready and able to become aware of, genuinely accept, and take action to respond rather than react to the occurrence of any form or extent of unappreciative more, better, different thinking.

Reflections

I first became aware of the efficacy of willingness early on in my participation in Workaholics Anonymous. Back then my sponsor, a seasoned recovering workaholic, suggested that I "pray for the willingness to do nothing." At first, I misunderstood his direction. I thought he meant that I should pray for and literally do nothing whatsoever. So I attempted to comply by forcing myself to sit alone for extended periods of time without saying or doing anything at all. But no matter how many times or how hard I prayed and tried, this effort ended up increasing rather than decreasing the unease and other degrees of deep discontent that were my constant companions at that time.

But a short while later, it dawned on me that "willingness" was the operative word in my sponsor's instructions. I realized that he wasn't suggesting that I actually do nothing, but rather, he was offering me a way to bring forth the readiness—the willingness—needed for me to make further progress in my recovery from work addiction.

About a year later, the efficacy of willingness became even more apparent to me when my mother angrily accused me of being a "changeling." She meant this in a derogatory way, judging me a weakling because of my changed attitude towards work. However, even at that time I strongly sensed that being a changeling was a good thing, a positive attribute. Had I not had the willingness to change my thinking and behavior in relation to work, it's hard to imagine that I would have happened upon the practice of contentment not to mention the countless other wonderful aspects of my post-breakout life. This is why just yesterday a big smile came to my face while listening to an audio presentation, *A Walk Through The Presence Process*, by the South African author Michael Brown. I heard him say, "In every family there is born an individual or sometimes two individuals who we would call the black sheep of the family [but] is really the transformer in the family [or] as I call it the 'changeling'… the only one who can make real changes in the dysfunctional patterns in the family… [and] get to a point of awareness where they can transform themselves…"

Today I definitely know that although there may be times when willingness is born from a particularly painful experience, such as the intense dread I felt when first submitting to in-patient treatment, there are other times when it can arise from a strongly felt premonition that moving forward with something will ultimately be for the good. For example, from sheer happenstance or even grace, my willingness during treatment led to my being able to change the dysfunctional patterns in my family and model very different behaviors for my children than those that were modeled for me. Similarly, willingness has continually provided the internal energy I needed to write this book with patience. Through all these experiences, I consider myself truly blessed to have had and continue to have the willingness to be a "changeling."

Chapter 5

The Origins of More, Better, Different Thinking

*"The mind is its own place, and in itself
can make a heaven of Hell, a hell of Heaven."*
John Milton[7]

Becoming aware of the origins of our not-enough thoughts—our ideas, opinions, beliefs, evaluations, judgments, and the like—is fundamental to the practice of contentment. Without such awareness we will continue to suffer several harmful consequences: (1) We will repeatedly fall prey to the delusion—the misconception of the mind—that we can't be content unless we acquire and achieve an excess of more, better, and different things; (2) We will time and again mistakenly believe that there is something inherently bad, wrong, or immoral about the occurrence of not-enough thinking; and (3) We will continually suffer the negative emotional and behavioral outcomes of this delusional type of thinking. Given these harms, practitioners of contentment must become and then remain aware of the origins of their thoughts

---

[7] The 17th Century English poet and historian who is best known for his epic poem, *Paradise Lost*.

in general and their unappreciative more, better, different ones in particular.

Our thoughts originate from our sense perceptions: how we interpret what we see, hear, touch, taste and smell. Like a spider building its web, the left and right hemispheres of our brain (i.e., our mind) weave a complex tapestry of perceptions which subsequently inform our thoughts, each of them intricately interconnecting and overlapping with one another.

The perceptions that inform our more, better, different thoughts originate in the left hemisphere of our brain. This is the analytical and objective side of our mind which separates and organizes our sensory experiences into safe-dangerous, good-bad, right-wrong and other divisions in accordance with our particular genetic constitution as well as our individual, familial and cultural conditioning.

The right hemisphere of our brain is very different from the left one. It is the intuitive and subjective side of our mind. It receives experiences without categorization or division.

The left hemisphere houses our *ego*: those of our subconsciously stored memories which inform our sense of self. Our ego contributes to our self-identity and self-worth based on the ways in which we have labeled and evaluated ourselves beginning in early childhood.

On one hand, our ego functions to safeguard us against psychological and physical harm. On the other hand, it creates delusions—misconceptions of the mind which create false or mistaken beliefs about ourselves, our circumstances, and reality—which obscure and prevent (if not completely preclude) our ability to see things as they really are.

One of these misconceptions of the mind is the delusion of separation. This mistaken perception deceives us into believing that we are separate from one another and detached from everything else despite the scientifically proven fact that everyone and everything is inseparably part of an infinitely vast interconnected energetic network, much like a wave is an inseparable part of the ocean.

Similarly, the delusion of permanence is another misconception of the mind created by our ego. While science shows us that everything is impermanent and perpetually changing, down to each cell in our body, the delusion of permanence leads us to mistakenly believe that we will never change.

These misconceptions of the mind further include the delusion of time, the persistent albeit mistaken belief that there is a difference between the past, the present, and the future. In truth, according to no lesser an authority than Albert Einstein, "the distinction between past, present, and future is only a stubbornly persistent illusion" (with an illusion being a very close cousin of a delusion, both of which are based on false beliefs).

Clearly, any and all forms of delusion distort reality, some to a greater extent than others. They are all mind-made misconceptions which create internal conflict, dissonance between what we mistakenly believe to be true and what is actually true. As such, these delusional beliefs inevitably cause us to experience bodily reactions in the form of anxiety, angst and myriad other dimensions of discontent.

In practical terms, however, there isn't much we can do to avoid the internal conflict created by those delusions. Because delusions such as those of separation, permanence, and time are deeply embedded in our psyche, it's virtually impossible to consistently remain aware of these misconceptions, much less psychologically deal with the reality that we are all inextricably interconnected, changing from one impermanent form to another, and existing in a timeless universe.

Thankfully, the delusion that contentment can come from the acquisition or achievement of more, better, and different things is closer to the surface of our psyche. As such, it is easier to remain consistently aware of its occurrence and, therefore, it is also easier to quell the internal conflict it creates.

It is fundamental that practitioners of contentment remain aware of both the adaptive and maladaptive functions of the left hemisphere of the brain. One on hand, this part of the mind can help us cope with such realities as our own impermanence and inevitable death, but conversely it may also lead us to fall prey to the dissatisfaction, dismay and other dimensions of discontent that derive from the delusion that an excess of more, better, and different things can make us content.

It is equally important that a practitioner remember that there is nothing inherently bad, wrong or immoral about the occurrence of unappreciative more, better, different thinking. He or she must steadfastly remain aware that these types of thoughts are natural products of the ways in which the left side of the brain is structured and functions. We are hardwired to have these types of thoughts. On one hand such perceptions have been and continue to be indispensable to our survival as a species, providing us with the wherewithal to navigate through an ever-changing and sometimes dangerous world as well as giving us the motivation to make countless life-enhancing advances in medicine, science, and technology. Yet on the other hand, these types of thoughts are also the source of a great deal of discontent. For example, humankind has almost continuously inflicted immense suffering on itself by waging wars about which nation, religion, or economic system is more, better, or different than another.

Reflections

Given this way in which our minds are structured and function, it's not surprising that, no matter how much we already have, most of us will continue to seek an even greater excess of more, better, and different things. Nor is it surprising that most of us will continue to judge and compare ourselves to others. We continuously judge ourselves as being or having more or less, better or worse, and different or the same as someone else. We compare ourselves to other people who appear to have more money, better relationships, different careers, and so on, rather than those who appear to have less, repeatedly comparing our insides to someone else's ostensibly more, better or different outsides. In the absence of awareness about not-enough thinking, these endless comparisons will inevitably lead to increasingly deeper dimensions of discontent.

Truth be told, to this day I still sometimes have to remind myself that even my most shameful judgments, jealous comparisons, and other types of equally abhorrent unappreciative thoughts are common and normal; that their periodic occurrence doesn't mean that I am irreparably damaged. That even though I already have my fair share of loved ones and close friends, good health, material possessions and career accomplishments, the occurrence of not-enough thinking is a fact of life.

Take, for instance, my recurrent not-enough thoughts about money, which still periodically surface and generate discontent. Even though my wife and I have an above average amount of money, I still periodically slip into unappreciative thinking about our financial condition, all too often picturing our glass as half-empty rather than half-full. On an intellectual level, I completely understand that these not-enough thoughts result from the ways in which my brain is structured and has been conditioned, but I still occasionally slip into judging myself as greedy or in some other way fundamentally flawed for not appreciating all that I already have.

That said, I am long past blaming anybody or anything else for these not-enough thoughts and the discontent they evoke. I am now sufficiently aware of the origins of my not-enough thoughts to know that it is the development of a predominately appreciative state of mind, not more money or anything else, which gives rise to contentment.

Chapter 6

The Nature of Unappreciative More, Better, Different Thoughts

"There is nothing either good or bad,
but thinking makes it so."
William Shakespeare[8]

In addition to being delusional, unappreciative more, better, different thinking is also fantastical and fictional in nature. Not-enough thinking is inherently fantastical because it is pure fantasy to believe that any amount or type of possession or achievement, or any kind of someone else, can make us content. In reality this belief only exists in our imagination, frequently taking the form of *if only* and *could of, would have, should have* not-enough kinds of thoughts.

Sadly, most of us nevertheless regularly indulge in fantastical not-enough thinking about the past and future. We conjure up mental imaginings about how our life could or should have been or would be more, better and different: *If only my mother had been more understanding... If only I was better at sticking up for myself... If only I could get a different job.* We repetitively ruminate on these

---

[8] The renowned poet, playwright and actor who is regarded as the greatest writer in the English language.

fantastical wishes as if they could dissolve our discontent, when in reality they can only deepen it.

Our not-enough thoughts are also fictional in nature because they are nothing more than mind-made interpretations and imaginings. They are make-believe stories we tell ourselves based on our subjective interpretations of what wasn't enough for us in the past or what we speculate will or will not be enough for us in the future.

Unfortunately, the vast majority of us spend an inordinate amount of time inside of our heads shaping and reshaping our not-enough fictional stories, despite the fact that the composition of the thoughts that inform these stories have little if any basis in objective reality. The succeeding feelings generated by these stories make us momentarily less discontent or perhaps even happy, only to subsequently sway us to fall back into the same or even a deeper degree of discontent from where we started. Like Sisyphus in Greek mythology, who was punished for his deceitfulness with the task of unendingly rolling a huge boulder up a hill only to watch it time and again roll back down, we repeatedly punish ourselves by trying to use our fictional not-enough thoughts to roll back the past or roll into the future, only to watch ourselves time and again suffer in vain one or another degree of discontent.

Therefore, the delusional, fantastical and fictional character of our unappreciative more, better, different thoughts adds to the necessity that practitioners of contentment become aware of the nature of unappreciative thinking. To have any chance of experiencing increasingly frequent and longer lasting moments of contentment, we must steadfastly remain aware of their decidedly deceitful, unrealistically wishful, and inherently make-believe nature.

Reflections

Before the practice of contentment, I certainly had my share of delusional, fantastical, and fictional not-enough thoughts. For example, I was plagued with persistent *if only* and *should, would, and could have* thoughts for several years after selling my interest in the law firm I founded.

It took over seventeen years to build my law firm which disintegrated in less than six months after two large groups of lawyers resigned to form their own firms. I was shocked by this disintegration, to say the least, so much so that I sold my interest to my remaining partners in the following year and took over the management of my parents' company.

During the next few years I was periodically beleaguered with delusional, fantastical and fictional thoughts about this disintegration. Not-enough thoughts would suddenly pop up such as, *if only I could or would have done such and such, than things would have developed more to my liking,* and, *I should or could have done this, or I shouldn't have done that, so things would have turned out better and differently.*

When looking back on these events now, I realize that the anguish and other degrees of discontent I felt was a direct result of my lack of knowledge about the delusional, fantastical and fictional nature of not-enough thinking. I also appreciate that my discontent was largely, albeit subconsciously, self-inflicted. Had I been aware of the true nature of this not-enough *if only*, *could have*, and *should or shouldn't have* thinking, I would have been able to minimize my suffering.

So, William Shakespeare had it right when he said "there is nothing either good or bad, but thinking makes it so." There was nothing inherently good or bad about my law firm's disintegration; it was my lack of awareness about not-enough thinking that made it feel bad to me. In fact, as with so many other events in my life which initially seemed bad or even catastrophic, the disintegration of my law firm turned out to be a blessing in disguise, an event which gave me the opportunity to take a very different direction in my life than that in which I was headed. At the time, this different direction was not the one that I *wanted* to take, but I now realize that it was definitely the one which I *needed* to take to become the person I am today: someone who likes who and what he is; or, in the context of this book, someone who has his fair share of the natural wealth of contentment.

Chapter 7

The Circularity of More, Better, Different Thinking Energy

"Our minds influence the key activity of the brain, which then influences everything: perception, cognition, thoughts and feelings, personal relationships."
Deepak Chopra[9]

As I mentioned before, all of our thoughts originate from our perceptions. These are our moment-by-moment observations and interpretations of our sensory experiences: what we see, touch, hear, taste and smell. The myriad ways in which our brains process the complex electrochemical events that result from our perceptions are beyond the scope of this book. For the purpose of practicing contentment, it is sufficient to know that these events generate our thoughts, which thereupon in sequence trigger our emotions, influence our behavior, alter our earlier perceptions, and give birth to new thoughts. This sequential process continues in a cyclical manner,

---

[9] The contemporary Indian-born American medical doctor, author and public speaker who advocates for alternative medicine and the connection between the mind and the body.

with the internal energy of these events continually looping around and around in circles.

The circularity of this process and associated internal energy shape our brain and ease the passage of the same or similar thoughts, carving new or reinforcing existing neural pathways with each experience. Like the force of the ancient glaciers that carved the contours of our planet, the force of the internal energy produced by how we perceived our previous experiences carved the contours of our brains.

Fortunately, our brains are remarkably malleable. In fact, according to contemporary neuroscience the brain has the capacity—the neuroplasticity—to continually grow and change. Therefore it's never too late for us to reshape the contours of our brain by intentionally carving new neuronal pathways.

So, you might ask, what does this circularity of internal energy and plasticity of the brain have to do with the practice of contentment? The answer is that we can actually change the contours of our brain by practicing contentment. By intentionally focusing our awareness on any discontent we feel and ferreting out the not-enough thought that preceded it, we can put the energy of our emotions in service of changing the nature of the thoughts which predominately populate our mind at any given moment. We can purposefully take advantage of our brain's malleability to incrementally carve neural pathways for the transmission of appreciative thoughts. After all, we can't see the picture when we're inside the frame, so we can't see the not-enough picture painted by our perceptions and thoughts until we step out of the discontent they evoked by noticing it.

Consequently, the discontent resulting from our not-enough thoughts is the pivotal point in this circularity. It's crucial for practitioners of contentment to steadfastly strive to be aware of any degree of discontent they feel so as to interrupt this circularity at the point it surfaces as one of the bodily reactions we associate with discontent. Unlike our perceptions, we are aware of these bodily reactions and can therefore see the not-enough thoughts that induced them. It is in this way that practitioners of contentment can change the behavior that follows unappreciative thinking and thereby set a circular energy in motion that will create contentment rather than discontentment.

Reflections

It was while I was exploring the nexus between happiness and expectations that I first realized how our perceptions, thoughts, feelings and behaviors cycle in circular loops. However, it wasn't until developing the concepts underlying the practice of contentment that I realized the importance of firmly focusing on my feelings so as to interrupt this circularity and expose the not-enough thought behind it. It wasn't important for me to trace my feelings all the way back to the perception that informed my thought, which I am not sure is even possible to do. The important task is to uncover the secondary source of my discontent: the unappreciative more, better, different thought that evoked it.

It became obvious to me that there was no other way to be cognizant of the occurrence of not-enough thinking. Without stepping out of the frame constructed by my perception of the circumstance which gave rise to my unappreciative thinking, there would be no opportunity to mentally trace my discontent back to its secondary source—which is an essential step in the practice of contentment.

Am I perfect in stepping out of this frame these days? Of course not. Sometimes I'm oblivious to having been discontent. Other times I'm aware of it but pay it no heed, too busy or too lazy to mentally search for the not-enough thought behind it.

However, when I do take the time and expend the effort to pay attention to any dimension of discontent I experience and ferret out the not-enough thought that preceded it, I always feel at least some measure of contentment. And then my behavior follows suit. I am no longer a slave to my not-enough thoughts, forced to do their misguided bidding. I am free to select whatever action will set up a flow of internal energy which will change the contours of my mind and make it increasingly easier for me to realize the serenity and satisfaction characteristic of contentment.

Chapter 8

The Negative Emotional Consequences of Not-Enough Thinking

"I believe that we are solely responsible for our choices, and we have to accept the consequences of every deed, word, and thought throughout our lifetime."
Elisabeth Kubler-Ross[10]

The **negative emotional** consequences of unappreciative more, better, different thinking can show up in the form of mad, bad, or sad feelings. Other times they can take the shape of much stronger emotions, such as disabling fear and insatiable desire. Irrespective of how and to what degree these consequences manifest, they can and most likely will bring about a plethora of unhelpful and unproductive, if not destructive or even dangerous, emotional consequences when we remain unaware of them.

However, as they say, "forewarned is forearmed." When we are aware of the emotionally negative

---

[10] The late Swiss-American psychiatrist and groundbreaking author who in her book, On Death and Dying (1969), articulated the five stages of grief we go through when facing death.

consequences of our not-enough thinking described below, we will be forewarned about them and thus forearmed to avoid or at least lessen their negative outcomes. Our awareness of them will raise red flags, warning signs which afford us the opportunity to transform these types of thoughts into harbingers of contentment instead of discontentment.

Mad, Bad, Sad Feelings

"Pain is inevitable, suffering is optional."
Buddhist Proverb

Mad, bad and sad are generic labels for the myriad shapes and sizes of discontent that derive from not-enough thinking. They are catchall words used for a range of emotions we experience as discontent. The spectrum of discontent is broad, with the discontent that we call "mad" ranging in intensity from feeling mildly annoyed to extremely angry; the discontent that we refer to as "bad" varying in strength from feeling slightly out of sorts to severely shattered; and the discontent that we label as "sad" extending from feeling somewhat down to deeply depressed.

The intensity of the discontented feelings generated by not-enough thinking is determined by the extent to which we are "identified" with it. It is also determined by the degree we are "attached" to acquiring or achieving the thing that a not-enough thought deluded us into believing would make us content.

Our identification with our thoughts is largely founded on the paradigm expounded by the eminent 17th Century French philosopher and mathematician René Descartes: "I think therefore I am." This model continues to primarily inform our Western beliefs about who and what we are, shaping our self-identity. Given that we define ourselves this way, there is little wonder why the vast majority of us are so inextricably entwined with our not-enough thoughts that we actually, albeit inaccurately, believe we are one and the same as them. We become so caught up in these thoughts that they become our masters instead of the other way around—enslaving us to continually suffer one degree or another of their negative consequences.

Attachments form when we emotionally bond to another person or thing. It's common and normal for us to form attachments to other people, primarily our parents, and to those matters that we became emotionally invested in, such as our career or the outcome of a particular situation or event. But, apropos to the practice of contentment, it is the extent to which we have become attached to acquiring or achieving the subject matter of a not-enough thought that will determine the intensity of the mad, bad or sad feelings which ensue. If we are deeply attached to getting the subject matter of a not-enough thought, our discontent is likely to register at the higher levels of intensity. On the other hand, if the subject matter of an unappreciative thought is relatively unimportant to us, our discontent is likely to be of lower intensity, perhaps only barely registering on the mad, bad, sad scale of discontent.

Fortunately, even our most intense mad, bad, sad feelings typically diminish as we progress through the five-stage grief process identified by Dr. Elisabeth Kubler-Ross. This process is the non-linear emotional passage that Kubler-Ross posited we all go through when facing death: denial, anger, bargaining, depression and acceptance. This is also the emotional passage that most mental health professionals now widely recognize applies to less existential circumstances, such as when we lose a significant relationship due to death or divorce. In the practice of contentment, this emotional passage applies to the intensity of discontented feelings evoked by our not-enough thinking, which typically diminishes as we grieve and eventually come to terms with the reality that this type of thinking is part and parcel of our humanness.

Reflections

I imagine that by now it would come as no surprise that my identification with and attachment to my not-enough thoughts was particularly acute during the time when I was running my law firm and then my parents' company. Back then, I was so mentally identified with and emotionally attached to my not-enough thoughts with respect to work that there was no separation in my mind between who I was and the work-related roles I played in these enterprises. I was defined by my virtually non-stop unappreciative thoughts about these enterprises. I was caught up in the belief that I would never have enough clients and cases and, later on, enough customers and profits. These thoughts were me and I was them, with little if any separation between us.

Over the course of the first several years following my breakout, it became clearer and clearer to me that my discontent was a result of my identification with and attachment to these kinds of not-enough thoughts. I realized that I actually (albeit subconsciously) engineered the confluence of two sets of circumstances which first led to the disintegration of my law firm and later to my abrupt exit from my parents' company.

I really didn't fit into the roles I had been playing in these enterprises—a hardnosed trial attorney and senior partner of a commercial litigation law firm, and then a callous profit-driven manager and part-owner of a distribution company. Eventually, I came to understand that this disconnect between who I actually was and who I thought I *should be* was creating such strong discontent that I subconsciously conspired to bring about the exact sets of circumstances which left me with little choice but to separate from them. As expressed by the new testament biblical paradox, "He who shall save his life shall lose it, and he who shall lose his life shall save it," in each of these instances, I unwittingly set in motion the perfect storm of circumstances in which I had to "lose" the life I was living as a result of my identification with and attachment to not-enough thinking to be able to literally "save" my life. I have no doubt whatsoever that, had I remained in either of these roles, my discontent would have become so extreme that I would have created yet another set of circumstances which would have brought my discontent, or indeed my life, to an end in the form of a heart attack, fatal accident, or other terminal incident.

I am now well aware that I can make no further progress towards fully accepting my unappreciative more, better, different thoughts until I am able to sever my identification with and attachment to them. Likewise, I am also well aware that disidentifying and detaching from these thoughts is the way to set myself free from becoming mentally and emotionally entrenched in them—thus creating the opportunity for me to move forward to fully accreted acceptance of these types of thoughts.

Persistent Fear & Insatiable Desire

"Most people's lives are run by desire and fear."
Eckhart Tolle[11]

If you were to drill down deep into your psyche, you would discover that fear underlies all of the various mad, bad and sad feelings that are consequential to your unappreciative thoughts.

---

[11] A German-born Canadian who is currently a widely acclaimed author and spiritual teacher.

You would also discover that all the desires that stem from your not-enough thoughts are the flipside of the fear that derives from these types of thoughts. In other words, the persistent fears and insatiable desires generated by your not-enough thoughts are two sides of the same emotional coin.

All of the fears and desires generated by your not-enough thoughts are psychological, existing only in your mind as a result of your body's reaction to your mind. Thus, they are very different from the instinctual fears and desires we all have from our natural built-in instincts to seek pleasure and avoid pain. In the end, all of the fears and desires that derive from our unappreciative thinking are nothing other than products of our misguided mind-made belief that we need an excess of more, better, and different things to be content.

Sadly, until we become aware of our not-enough thinking and the psychological fears and desires it can produce, we will continue to go through life alternately anxious, worried and otherwise fearful, while also needy, greedy and likewise desirous of having more and more, better and better, and different upon different things. Like black holes in the universe, without awareness our not-enough thoughts will suck us out of the reality that we already have enough of everything necessary to meet our essential needs and be content, and push us into our own mind-made fear that we will never have enough to be content unless we acquire or achieve an excess of more, better and/or different things.

Most of us have already become so accustomed to the fears and desires that stem from our not-enough thoughts that we hardly notice them. They have become so familiar that we just shrug them off as common and normal, part of contemporary life. Indeed, as dysfunctional as it might seem, many of us actually take comfort in these fears and desires. We become so used to this unfortunate reality that we find it anxiety-evoking *not* to be persistently fearful and insatiably desirous of getting or achieving more, better and different things.

Reflections

Looking back on my workaholic years it's easy for me to see the huge extent to which my life was filled with unappreciative thinking and thus steeped in psychological fears and desires. At my law firm, I was constantly fraught with fear about not getting more and more clients while on the flipside single-mindedly driven by the desire to get an endless number of them. Later, while in charge of my parents' company, these fears and desires multiplied, devilishly driving me to greater and greater extents of not-enough fears and desires, no matter what the cost to my health and relationships. In fact, I was one of those people who actually felt anxious when I didn't have anything to fear. As crazy as it now seems, there was a period of time in which the only way I could fall to sleep at night was to intentionally think of something about which to worry.

Thankfully, I am now far less troubled by the fears and desires that stem from not-enough thinking.

For example, I now acknowledge that I suffered a series of traumatic childhood abandonment experiences which left me believing that I wasn't enough for my parents. With this awareness, I can readily assuage, if not entirely eliminate, the remnants of any mind-made fear I experience about being abandoned again as well as any desire I have to set myself up for another abandonment in order to prove (albeit dysfunctionally) that I'm really *not* enough.

Currently, I do my best to remember that any mad, bad, sad and other measure of discontent I feel is psychological, derived from my mind-made fear of not having or being enough along with my flipside mind-made desire to get or achieve a surfeit of more, better, and different things. For instance, when I become fearful of not having enough money and start thinking about how I could or should get more, I do my best to bring my awareness to the fact that these feelings are simply mind-made reactions to the arrival of a not-enough thought which I just had. As such, I can realize that they are purely psychological, not instinctual, with no basis in reality whatsoever.

Diminished Self-Esteem

"The worst loneliness is to
not be comfortable with yourself."

Mark Twain[12]

The persistent pursuit of more, better, or different non-essential things is sure to diminish our self-esteem: the subconscious beliefs and feelings we have about our own importance and worth as a person. After all, if we constantly fall victim to the bogus belief that a surplus of possessions and achievements will make us content, but each time wind up feeling the same or even deeper degrees of discontent, our self-esteem is bound to suffer. To paraphrase Mark Twain, we will suffer the "worst loneliness" and other deeply felt dimensions of discontent that come from being less and less comfortable with ourselves. In fact, when we constantly chase after the ill-conceived ends of our not-enough thoughts we unwittingly subject our self-esteem to something akin to the so-called *Chinese water torture.* Instead of water slowly dropping onto our foreheads and eventually driving us insane, our very own not-enough thoughts will slowly drop into our psyches, each time driving us to lower and lower levels of self-esteem.

Diminished self-esteem is thus another emotional consequence of unappreciative thinking. It is common for children and adolescents to suffer some decline in their self-esteem as they navigate and interpret their interactions with the world.

[12] The 19th Century renowned American who authored two major classics: The Adventures of Tom Sawyer and The Adventures of Huckleberry Finn.

But for many of us, it is our own not-enough thoughts and the mad, bad, sad, desirous and fearful feelings they generate that further diminish our self-esteem as we progress through life.

Commercial advertisements even further diminish our self-esteem with their insidious tactics. Whether in magazines and newspapers or on television and the internet, ads are carefully crafted to convey subliminal messages aimed at convincing us that our importance and worth as a person is dependent on getting the more, better or different thing being advertised. In this way commercial advertisers purposely want us to believe that getting their product will boost our self-esteem and thereby make us content—when quite the opposite is true.

As if the foregoing negative effects of our unappreciative thinking weren't sufficiently damaging to our self-esteem, a good number of us repeatedly go to great and perhaps even dangerous lengths to reinforce our beliefs and feelings that underneath it all we really are unimportant and unworthy. In this way, some may self-sabotage any chance of improving their self-esteem and contentment by unwittingly engaging in relationships and/or situations that have no real chance of succeeding. In fact, such relationships and situations actually serve to reinforce their subconscious beliefs and feelings of unimportance and unworthiness, further diminishing their self-esteem.

Reflections

I distinctly remember several childhood and adolescent experiences which contributed to my believing that I was unimportant and unworthy. These include several situations in which the actions of certain authority figures left me feeling stupid and not-enough as well as several instances when I was physically and emotionally abandoned by my parents. For many years now, it's been crystal clear to me that my self-esteem was already considerably diminished by the time I reached adulthood.

Despite having earned several advanced educational degrees, founded a prominent law firm, and acquired the accoutrements of wealth, underneath it all I still felt unimportant and unworthy compared to my peers. Indeed, I subconsciously created certain circumstances which actually reinforced these beliefs and feelings. For example, at my law firm I occasionally rod roughshod over certain associate attorneys as well as partners, only to ultimately have them leave the firm. I created the exact circumstances I deeply feared, proving to one and all, including myself, that I was not worthy enough for them to not abandon me. Similarly at my parents' company, I would try my best to intimidate any employee who didn't kowtow to my workaholic ways, all the while totally unaware of the self-sabotaging effects of overcompensating in these ways for my already diminished self-esteem.

It wasn't until about fifteen years ago when several events coalesced, including my mother and then my father disinheriting me, that my beliefs and feelings about myself began to reverse direction towards incrementally higher and higher levels of self-esteem. Ironically, it took these kinds of egregious experiences for me to finally realize that I am important and worthy—and deserve to be content!

Sore Spots

"Memory resides not just in brains but in every cell."
James Gleick[13]

Any and all of the foregoing negative emotional consequences of unappreciative more, better, different thinking cause the formation of "sore spots": tender tendrils of negative internal energy in our bodies. Like the not-enough thoughts stored in our brains, our bodies store the energy generated by these types of thoughts. Whether our discontent took the form of mad, bad, or sad feelings, the shape of disabling fear and insatiable desire, or the dimension of diminished self-esteem, our bodies stored the negative energy of these discontents on a cellular level.

Once stored, sore spots increase in size and strength with each new occurrence of the same or a similar not-enough thought. They amass in what Eckhart Tolle, in his best-selling book *The Power of*

---

[13] A contemporary best-selling American author and science historian.

Now, called a "pain-body": a "negative energy field...[composed of] the residue of pain... that becomes lodged in your mind and body...[that] anything can trigger... particularly if it resonates with a pain pattern from your past." They become increasingly tender. Much easier to trigger and inflame.

Some sore spots start out tenderer and thus easier to inflame than others. For example, the sore spot formed from a child having been physically abused by a parent is bound to be of much greater size and strength than most others. As young children we idealize our parents to such an overwhelming extent that it's impossible for us to believe that they can do any wrong. This being our reality, we subconsciously think that had we been more, better or different in this way or that, we wouldn't have been abused. We wind up blaming ourselves instead of them and unwittingly submerge the energy of the shame and other degrees of discontent we experienced as a result of this not-enough thinking—which thereupon lives on as an exceptionally sensitive sore spot, one that can be easily inflamed by any incident we perceive as being the same or even remotely related to our childhood abuse.

To add fuel to the inflammation derived from these cellular sore spots, scientific research has shown that our painful remembrances last much longer and are recalled in greater detail than our pleasurable ones. Sometimes referred to as a "negativity bias," this research suggests that unless we become aware of the arrival of an unappreciative thought, we will remain at risk of it forever inflaming one of our sore spots and thus generating yet another round of negative emotional consequences.

Our sore spots can, however, diminish in size and strength. As I will explain in Part Two, with the practice of contentment we can decrease their inflammation and resultant capacity to cause discontent.

Reflections

One of my particular sore spots formed when I was in the third grade, a time in my life in which I was so sickly and so slow to learn that my teacher told my parents that I should repeat that grade. Suffice it to say that my parents didn't take well to this and acted out in ways that left me thinking I was "stupid" and feeling ashamed—the negative energy of which formed a severely sensitive sore spot. From then until only about fifteen years ago (the circumstances of which I will recount later on), this sore spot would become instantaneously inflamed if anyone ever inferred, much less out rightly said, that I was stupid.

Another of my specific sore sports formed from the discontent I experienced when my law firm disintegrated. And yet another one formed from the anger and other aggressive forms of discontent I felt upon resigning from my parent's company. In fact I still feel a minor measure of mad, bad or sad when one of these sore spots is inflamed by some situation reminiscent of either of these events.

Currently, having practiced contentment for some time, I now know that the energy contained in these sore spots will never completely dissipate. My body will forever remember at least some degree of the discontent derived from my not-enough thinking in relation to these experiences as well as those that in the years to follow I perceived were akin to them. At the same time, however, I also now know that by practicing contentment I will be able to greatly reduce the likelihood that my sore spots will produce any of the negative behavioral consequences described in the next chapter.

Chapter 9

The Negative Behavioral Consequences of Not-Enough Thinking

"The negative side of the American Dream comes when people pursue success at any cost, which in turn destroys the vision and the dream."
Azar Nafisi[14]

Now that you are aware of the emotional consequences of unappreciative more, better, different thinking, it's time to become aware of its negative behavioral consequences. To be specific, it's time to understand that unless you become aware of your not-enough thoughts, the persistent fears and insatiable desires that underlie them will sooner or later produce one or more of the following undesirable and unproductive behaviors.

---

[14] An Iranian born American contemporary writer and professor.

Reflexive Reactions

"Have the courage to act instead of react."
Oliver Wendell Holmes, Sr.[15]

To react to not-enough thinking is to reflexively repeat the same or similar behavior over and again, while each time expecting more, better or different results. Whereas the early 20th century world-renowned Swiss psychiatrist, Carl Jung, believed that this type of reflexive behavior is indicative of insanity, here it indicates a lack of awareness about the behavioral consequences of not-enough thinking.

To react to our not-enough thoughts also indicates an unwillingness to take responsibility for our very own thinking. It may be true that we are powerless over the arrival of these types of thoughts; they seemingly come and go on their own. But, knowing that we are not helpless, all but a very few of us are capable of recognizing the irresponsibility implicit in robotically reacting rather than rationally responding to our not-enough thoughts. In other words, the vast majority of us know that when we act instead of react, we are able to consciously respond to the present day realities of a situation or event rather than

---

[15] A 19th Century American physician, poet, professor, lecturer, author, and father of the Justice of the United Supreme Court, Oliver Wendell Holmes, Jr.

reflexively react in a knee-jerk fashion to our old yet still there sore spots.

Finally, to react to our not-enough thoughts also denotes the ignorance of an unexamined mind; i.e., the mind of a person with very little or no awareness about the whys and wherefores of his or her thoughts and emotions, nor how they impact behavior. On the other hand, to respond signifies the wisdom of an examined mind; i.e., the mind of someone who is knowledgeable about the connection between his or her thoughts and emotions and how they affect actions.

Practitioners of contentment can and must free themselves from the insanity inherent in reflexively reacting rather than responsibly responding to the arrival of a not-enough thought. They must gain awareness which grants the introspective knowledge needed to recognize the connections between their thoughts, emotions and behaviors and provides them with the "courage to act instead of react." With this insight, we can find the courage to stand back from the pain of a sore spot which has been inflamed by a not-enough thought, knowing that in doing so we can avoid the negative behavioral consequences that would otherwise inevitably ensue. To find contentment, we must be steadfastly aware that continuing to mechanically march to the drumbeat of this type of thought would not only be irresponsible and ignorant but would most assuredly result in hurtful if not harmful behavior.

Reflections

There was a time when I was very much a reactor not a responder. I remember one instance in particular involving one of my law partners with whom I became increasingly angry because I thought he could have been doing much more, better and different in dealing with existing clients and bringing in new ones. I initially reacted to this instance of not-enough thinking by withdrawing, finding excuses to be out of the office so as to have as little contact with him as possible. But with each passing day I became increasingly discontent, indeed, angrier and angrier, and finally met with him—only to have my anger boil such that I uncontrollably ranted and raved at him like a three-year-old within hearing distance of several other attorneys and staff members.

Obviously, I reacted reflexively rather than responding responsibly. To say the least, it was not my finest moment! And to this day I still feel the echoes of embarrassment that resulted from the sore spot that had formed from my not-enough thinking about this law partner.

Yet, I'm also grateful for these kinds of echoes. They are helpful reminders that I must take responsibility for the anger and aggression (if not insanity) that can result from my not-enough thinking. They help me remember to take to heart what Thomas Jefferson said in this regard: "When angry count to ten before you speak; if very angry a hundred," and thereby avoid a lot of damage to myself and others. Additionally, these echoes, along with others from times when I reflexively reacted, afford me the time needed to trace whatever measure of anger or other degree of discontent I experience at any particular moment back to the not-enough thought that preceded it, thereby providing the knowledge needed for me to be able to rationally respond rather than reflexively react.

Flawed Relationships

"Some of the biggest challenges in relationships come from the fact that most people enter a relationship
in order to get something: they're trying to find someone who's going to make them feel good."
Anthony Robbins[16]

Like cracks that flaw the foundation of a building, not-enough thoughts flaw the foundation of relationships. Most people who enter into a relationship are "trying to find someone who's going to make them feel good." Since virtually everyone's self-esteem has been diminished by not-enough thinking, it is common that relationships are foundationally flawed.

Initially these cracks may be invisible. For example, it is especially common that our vision becomes blurred or even blocked by the novelty of a new romantic relationship. We may get caught

---

[16] A contemporary American motivational speaker and self-help author.

up in the excitement of being with a new person and fail to clearly assess the full situation.

But these cracks are sure to become increasingly visible as we settle into a relationship. One or both people will inevitably become disappointed, dissatisfied, disenchanted and otherwise discontented as a result of some sore spots having been ignited, leading them to act out in relationship-damaging, if not destroying, ways. They might withdraw from the relationship; perhaps they misguidedly search for contentment through extramarital affairs, alcohol or drugs while mentally and emotionally checking out of the partnership.

Their discontent may devolve into depression. Like a deer caught in the headlights of a car, a person stuck in not-enough thinking may be incapable of deciding whether to move closer or farther away from the relationship. Alternatively, one partner might blame his discontent on the other person in the relationship, mistakenly believing that he would be content—his sore spot would be soothed—if only the other person were somehow more, better or different.

Similar to Don Quixote in Miguel de Cervantes Saavedra's novel, *The Ingenious Gentleman Don Quixote of La Mancha*, who delusionally searched for chivalry by jousting with windmills, a person trapped in the pain of a sore spot derived from unappreciative discontent will delusionally search over and over for contentment in ways that further flaw his relationships instead of looking within himself to illuminate the not-enough thoughts behind his discontent. He won't understand that only he can do the inside job of dispelling the delusion that someone or something more, better, or different will make him content.

Reflections

The sore spots which form from unappreciative thinking are so pervasive that it is hard to imagine any relationship which isn't foundationally flawed by them to some degree. For centuries we have been thoroughly conditioned to believe that we cannot live, let alone be content, without finding someone who will supply the more, better, different things that will mend the cracks created by our predominately unappreciative state of mind. An early example of this conditioning is William Shakespeare's 15th century play, *Romeo and Juliette*, in which Romeo chose death over living without Juliette to make him feel content. A contemporary example is Mariah Carey's song, *I Can't Live without You*, in which she laments, "I can't live, if living is without you..." Of course she could technically "live," her heart wouldn't stop beating. But the underlying message of this song is that one can't be content without a "you" in one's life.

It wasn't until many years after my breakout that I finally understood how so many of my past relationships had been fundamentally flawed by the sore spots formed by my not-enough thinking. I was totally in the dark about how I unknowingly carried my diminished self-esteem into my personal and business relationships. I didn't realize that it was my own not-enough thoughts about myself which had progressively diminished my self-esteem and created the inevitable degrees of discontent that were initially invisible. but eventually became all too apparent in my relationships. Nor did I know that it was impossible to build a durable relationship founded on the recurrent not-enough thoughts which I had back then. My mind was filled with thoughts such as: *I am not important enough, intelligent enough, worthy enough or loveable enough*. One area where this discontent manifested was in my romantic relationships. I dated heavily in the years between my two marriages and, as the song from the movie *Urban Cowboy* goes, kept "looking for love in all the wrong places." Like Don Quixote, I repeatedly searched in vain for that special someone who would sooth my sore spots and make me content.

I was just plain lucky to meet, marry and have a now long-term caring, loving and mutually respectful relationship with my second wife. In the beginning of our relationship, I had no idea that she shared my not-enoughness. Like me at that time, she outwardly projected confidence and competence while inwardly thinking that she was unworthy, unintelligent and otherwise not enough. It took many years for me to realize that my sense of sufficiency in the relationship stemmed primarily from the fact that she was thirteen years younger, not as formally educated, and less worldly-wise. This allowed me to feel like I was truly *enough* with and for her.

My relationship with my wife was and continues to be living proof for over thirty years now that it is definitely possible to substantially mend most of the foundational not-enough cracks in a relationship. Or, in other words, that it is entirely possible to largely lessen the intensity of the sore spots that flaw relationships.

Looking back I can see that this mending process began immediately after my breakout. Before then, my wife and I did a pretty good job of covering up the cracks underneath the façade of confidence and competence which each of us had constructed. But afterwards, bits and pieces of these façades crumbled as each of us in our own way went through the arduous and occasionally acrimonious process of uncovering and mending these cracks. Our relationship was really rocky for a while, but this uncovering process turned out to be well worth it. We emerged from this experience with fresh insight and subsequently did our best to keep whatever cracks we become aware of in plain sight: visible for introspection, open for discussion, and ready for reconstruction.

Each of us grew increasingly self-assured that we are worth enough, smart enough and overall quite enough to deserve increasingly frequent and longer lasting moments of contentment—both individually and in relation to each other. We may not have pristinely patched all of the cracks in the foundation of our relationship, but we have both grown secure in our ability to develop a mostly appreciative state of mind about ourselves and each other. This state of mind not only strengthens our individual contentment but also allows our relationship to become even stronger and closer.

The business associations I had before my breakout also illustrate how the sore spots produced by not-enough thinking foundationally flaw relationships. Like my personal relationships, the cracks in these connections were initially invisible. For instance, even though I was the founder and principal owner of my law firm, when push came to shove I would typically defer to whichever one of my law partners I reckoned was smarter or in some other way better than me. I didn't realize that this way of thinking and behaving not only further diminished my self-esteem but also irritated my sore spots and widened the foundational cracks in these relationships, thereby making it inevitable that these partners would leave and form their own firms.

Until we become aware of the origins, nature and consequences of our not-enough thoughts, we are doomed to continually enter into relationships "to get something" that is impossible for anyone or something else to give us. We will continue to search for a balm to relieve the sore spots derived from our unappreciative discontent. I experienced the consequences of this lack of awareness when I married for the first time, dated heavily between marriages, and partnered with a series of different lawyers. As I discovered, we are likely to unwittingly engage in an unending succession of foundationally flawed relationships without any chance of mending the cracks caused by our not-enough thoughts until we become aware of the whys and wherefores of our unappreciative more, better, different thinking. It is this insight and awareness that allows us to patch the flaws, reduce the soreness, and stabilize the foundation of our relationships.

Materialism

"It is preoccupation with possessions,
more than anything else
that prevents us from living freely and nobly."
Henry David Thoreau[17]

We need only look at the recent "great recession" to see how devastating the materialism consequential to not-enough thinking can be. During this time, we witnessed how unbridled not-enough thinking by investment bankers and other lenders reached a critical mass, virtually bringing the whole world to the brink of economic disaster. We saw how the materialism spawned by our unappreciative thinking morphed what was once known as the "American Dream"—the possibility that everyone in America could attain prosperity and success—into a seemingly insatiable craving

---

[17] The 19th Century American renowned author, poet, philosopher, abolitionist, and historian who is best known for his book, Walden, in which he promoted the benefits of living simply in communion with nature.

for more and more, better and better, and different upon different material possessions.

These days the vast majority of Americans are no longer content to own a nice car, house, and so on. We have been so thoroughly conditioned by not-enough thinking that we remain discontent and our sore spots continue to fester no matter how many more, better and different things we already have. Consequently, most of us measure our wellbeing by the amount of possessions we have and continue to be compulsively driven by our not-enough thoughts. This compulsion to secure more and more brings an emotional, physical and personal price as well as inflicting environmental damage on our planet. Further, this drive to amass possessions brings increased worry, fear and other intensely sore spots concomitant to preserving and protecting them—all contributing to less contentment than before.

There seems to be no end in sight to the metastasization of our materialism. The vast majority of us are so obsessively and compulsively driven by unappreciative more, better, different thinking that a new word has been coined to describe our condition. *Affluenza*, a combination of the words *affluence* and *influenza*, has been created to reflect "a painful, contagious, socially transmitted condition of overload, debt, anxiety and waste resulting from the dogged pursuit of more."[18]

---

[18] Wikipedia

Reflections

Those of us living in the United States and other so-called "First World" countries have been persistently told by just about every mode of commercial advertising that we cannot possibly be happy, much less content, unless we have more of this, better of that, or something different. We are repeatedly bombarded with advertisements by radio, television, newspaper, magazine and internet which subliminally carry the message that we will remain unattractive, unmanly, unwanted, unsuccessful or similarly not-enough unless we get or attain whatever is being advertised. The primary purpose of such commercial advertising is to capitalize on our unappreciative more, better, different thinking.

We have similarly been incessantly bombarded with not-enough messages from our parents, teachers, bosses and other authority figures. Because they too were conditioned into not-enough thinking, they unknowingly taught us to highly regard and reward anyone who has obtained or achieved more, better and different things. Conversely we are trained to devalue those judged as lazy or incompetent. For instance, anyone who doesn't work at least fifty hours a week, wants extra time off, or just needs time to recuperate from having labored to the point of exhaustion is deemed less worthy of reward and admiration.

Sometimes the not-enough messages we receive are explicit, like when I was running my parents' company and harshly questioned my niece's work ethic after she asked for time off to care for her gravely ill grandmother. Other times these messages are implied. For example, a workplace colleague may mockingly judge a peer who is about to go home after putting in an eight-hour day by saying, "Oh, just working a half-time today, huh?" Still other times, a workplace is so thoroughly permeated with not-enough thinking that this belief system has become an intractable part of a company's culture. This is sadly the case in many corporations and professional firms, where employees are expected to work sixty-hour weeks and be available by phone, text and email no matter what time it is, where they are, or what they are doing. This was certainly my expectation when running my law firm. When I was in the midst of a trial and wanted something done by an associate attorney who was assigned to assist me, I never hesitated to insist that the associate do my bidding, irrespective of what time of day or night it was or how it would interfere with his or her personal life.

These days materialism has become so insinuated in most of our lives that it would be unrealistic to expect it to just fade away on its own. However, with practice and patience we can break free of its bondage. We can gradually reduce our cravings for an excess of more, better, and different material things and, in the process of doing so, begin to experience the satisfaction and serenity constituent of contentment.

Addiction

"The grasping or greed temperament is constructed around desire. It is experienced as a sense of seeking, of wanting more, and of addiction."
Jack Kornfield[19]

Any kind of addiction develops from the ways in which our bodies react to and store our experiences of anger, angst, dejection, depression and countless other degrees of discontent that can derive from not-enough thinking. They are all the result of the pain emanating from our sore spots. This is true of any kind of "substance" addiction which involves dependence on a chemical such as alcohol or a psychoactive drug. It is equally true of any kind of "behavioral" addiction which involves dependence on an activity such as gambling, eating, shopping, working or having sex.

Addiction denotes powerlessness: one's loss of control over a chemical or activity. Just as an alcoholic or cocaine addict cannot control his or her urge to ingest a substance, someone who has a behavioral addiction cannot control his or her urge to engage in a certain activity. Often, this desire begins as a *preference* for a particular pursuit which later degenerates into an obsessive and compulsive *need* for more and more of that substance or activity. The deep discontent derived

---

[19] The renowned contemporary American clinical psychologist, prolific author, and meditation teacher who co-founded the highly regarded Insight Meditation Society.

from the stored negative energy of not-enough thoughts pushes an individual to the point of no longer just *wanting* to ingest these substances or engage in these activities but rather of *needing* to get or do them. One can become so desperate to numb the pain caused by his sore spots that he will do whatever it takes regardless of the cost to himself or anyone else.

At first glance, it may seem relatively easy to break free of dependence on an activity as opposed to a substance. But, alas, this is not the case. In addition to dependence on an activity, behavioral addictions also involve dependence on two internally produced mind-altering drugs: adrenaline, an energy boosting chemical released by our adrenal glands; endorphins, pain killing chemicals secreted by our pituitary glands. Further contributing to the complex nature of behavioral addictions, we build up a tolerance to any kind of chemical substance with frequent use, including adrenaline and endorphins. This means that the anesthetizing effects of these chemicals diminish over time, such that we need to keep engaging in greater and greater extents of the behavior to which we are addicted to ward off the pain we would otherwise feel from our sore spots.

Therefore the primary purpose of any addiction is to self-medicate against the pain emanating from our sore spots. We use such dependencies as an attempt, albeit self-destructive, to gain some control over the pain ignited within a sore spot with every new occurrence of the same or a similar not-enough thought. Once addicted, we keep using a psychoactive substance or engaging in a certain activity to find relief from our painful sore spots, despite the reality that doing so will only deepen our discontent and addiction as well. Like someone who keeps going to the hardware store to buy milk, a person who is addicted to a substance or activity continues to reactively chase that pursuit in order to buy relief from the pain of the sore spots derived from his unappreciative thinking.

Reflections

Looking back, it's abundantly clear that I occasionally used mind-altering drugs and consistently engaged in various work activities in an attempt to quell the pain I would have otherwise experienced from the sore spots formed from not-enough thinking throughout my life. My behavioral addiction to work began at age twelve with my first job selling Christmas cards and persisted throughout my many part-time jobs during high school, college and law school and while at my law firm and parents' company. I used work to self-medicate against the mental, emotional and sometimes even physical pain I was otherwise unable to bear. I now realize that I kept working harder and harder, not as "preference" but, as a "need" for larger and larger doses of anesthetizing adrenaline and endorphins.

My behavior followed suit. In law school I would spend days on end studying by myself without any concern whatsoever for what my then-wife was doing much less feeling. As a practicing lawyer, I would sneak away from my wife, children and friends to snatch a few minutes of work in my home office when I could have been socializing. When running my parents' company, I would lie to my wife about the real reason why I was late coming home yet again: the chemically induced sense of calm and control I felt while at work. As is common with any addict, I would do whatever it took to get my fix. I would do anything that would let me avoid the painful degrees of discontent I would have otherwise had to deal with, even if it would disrupt or even damage other aspects of my life or relationships. It was in all of these ways that I was powerless over work. My addiction progressed to the point where I lost all control over the compulsion to work. I became a slave to the sore spots behind my workaholic behaviors, reflexively reacting to them in self-destructive and relationship-damaging ways.

While I was easily able to break free from my dependence on psychoactive drugs, it took quite a bit more time and energy for my dependence on work activities to subside. However after long-term participation in Workaholics Anonymous and Al-Anon meetings, individual psychotherapy and involvement in several different religious organizations and spiritual groups, I now rarely crave the adrenaline and endorphin "high" I used to get from engaging in work activities.

I still enjoy working, especially in my now over twenty -year career as a mediator. It's now something that I *prefer* not *need* to do, along with my many other activities including getting together with family and friends, painting with watercolors and acrylics, meditating, exercising, reading novels and spiritual books, and, last but not least, practicing and writing about contentment.

Sickness

"In order to change we must be
sick and tired of being sick and tired."
Anonymous

The sicknesses consequential to not-enough thinking can manifest in myriad mental and physical ways. They can also show up in different measures and mixtures. But no matter how and to what magnitude they appear, stress is central to every one of them.

According to the highly respected Mayo Clinic, "Long-term exposure to stress can lead to serious health problems. Chronic stress disrupts nearly every system in your body. It can raise blood pressure, suppress the immune system, increase the risk of heart attack and stroke, contribute to infertility, and speed up the aging process. Long-term stress can even rewire the brain, leaving you more vulnerable to anxiety and depression."

We cannot help but be stressed by the mad, bad, sad, fearful and desirous emotions that are consequential to not-enough thinking in the absence of awareness and acceptance. Nor can we help but be stressed by having to constantly cope with the diminished self-esteem and sore spots that develop from this kind of thinking.

For some of us, the stress consequential to our not-enough thoughts is alone sufficient to cause a great number of different illnesses. When added to the countless other stressors that most of us typically encounter in our everyday lives, the sustained stress we suffer from the repeated incidence of not-enough thoughts and the negative behaviors they produce are certain to cause virtually everyone, even the strongest and healthiest among us, to suffer one or perhaps even several forms of mental and physical sickness.

Spiritual sickness is another common negative consequence of not-enough thinking and the painful sore spots it causes. It is abundantly clear that the persistent pursuit of an excess of more, better and different possessions is a long-standing form of spiritual sickness. From Moses smashing the tablet containing the Ten Commandments upon seeing that the Israelites had built a golden alter, to Jesus pronouncing "Blessed are the poor," to Mohammad criticizing cultures which place excessive value on money and material goods, to Shakyamuni Buddha teaching about the life-diminishing dangers of becoming attached to material possessions, we repeatedly see warnings from spiritual leaders about the destructive consequences of a compulsive drive to attain more, better and different things.

Reflections

Even at the height of my workaholism, I regularly exercised and went out of my way to eat healthy food. I didn't realize it at the time, but these endeavors supported me in coping with the stress of persistently pursuing the bogus ends of my not-enough thoughts. While these healthy lifestyle habits took the edge off the stress of having to consistently sooth my sore spots, they were not enough to prevent the physical and psychological sicknesses I faced back then.

The stress caused by my not-enough thinking and ensuing workaholic behavior manifested in a variety of ways. For example, studies show those with highly stressful occupations, such as race car drivers, have extremely high cholesterol levels. My exceedingly high cholesterol levels were definitely consequential to the long-term stress spawned by my not-enough thinking and resultant workaholic behaviors. My recurrent dental problems were also manifestations of the stress attendant to my not-enough thinking. Indeed, on one occasion the stress I experienced from the prospect of not being able to work was so great that I coerced a dentist into pulling an impaired tooth rather than taking the time to save it. Similarly, my periodic anxiety attacks were further manifestations of my obsessive behaviors under stress and my inability to constructively cope with it at the time.

The stress consequent to not-enough thinking and resulting sore spots can also manifest in spiritual sickness. Early on in my involvement with 12-Step programs, I learned to describe this kind of illness as "spiritual bankruptcy": the condition of someone who has completely lost his or her connection with "the God of their understanding." Before my breakout I certainly belonged in that "lost" group of people, having been alternately agnostic and atheistic for most of my adult life. But, beginning with the spiritual awakening that occurred concurrently with my breakout and then over the course of the years that followed, I developed a robust relationship with the God of my understanding along with an abiding affinity to the non-theistic practices of Buddhism.

These days I am well aware of the countless physical, mental and spiritual sicknesses that can surface from the stress caused by unappreciative more, better, different thinking, the sore spots that it causes, and the behaviors that result from it. I do my best to alleviate and perhaps even eliminate the stress which can lead to these illnesses by first getting in touch with the not-enough thought that preceded it and then taking the second step in the practice of contentment: acceptance.

Part Two
ACCEPTANCE

"The first step toward change is awareness.
The second step is acceptance."
Nathaniel Branden[20]

---

[20] The late 20th Century Canadian-American psychotherapist and widely-read author best known for his writings about self-esteem.

Chapter 10

The Significance of Acceptance

"We cannot change anything until we accept it."
Carl Gustav Jung[21]

Congratulations! You are now aware of the origins and nature of unappreciative more, better, different thinking. You have also become knowledgeable about the similarities and differences between contentment and discontentment as well as those between contentment and happiness. With your growing understanding of the nature of your not-enough thoughts and how the internal energy they produce informs your perceptions, thoughts, feelings and behavior in circular sequences, you are becoming a practitioner of contentment!

As part of this journey, you have also become aware of the negative emotional and behavioral consequences that can happen when you reflexively react rather than responsibly respond to the occurrence of a not-enough thought. These types of thoughts will generate myriad mad, bad and sad feelings, persistent fears and insatiable desires for so long as you remain unaware of them.

---

[21] The 19th Century psychiatrist who established the idea of analytic psychology.

As you have discovered, this destructive cycle can diminish your self-esteem and form internal sore spots. When these sore spots become repeatedly inflamed by your discontentment, they lead you to unproductive behaviors such as engaging in reflexive reactions, fundamentally flawed relationships, materialism, addiction and sickness.

You have now reached the point in this practice where it's imperative that you understand the significance of acceptance in the practice of contentment. You must come to know that acceptance—the coming to terms with the occurrence of unappreciative more, better, different thinking—cannot transpire unless you are knowledgeable about and capable of processing through its constituents: acknowledgment, surrender and forgiveness.

By comprehending the significance of acceptance and practicing its constituents, you will experience firsthand how acceptance neutralizes the emotional sore spots consequential to unappreciative thinking while simultaneously causing the formation of "sweet spots": internal energy fields which are devoid of unappreciative more, better, different thinking and thus receptive to the infusion of thoughts which are appreciative in nature. These sweet spots are the kinds of internal energy fields which are ripe to receive the sweetness of life implicit in contentment. They are fertile fields, receptive to the sowing of seeds of thoughts which are appreciative instead of unappreciative in nature. Seeds which can take root and grow in size and strength each time you accept the advent of the same or similar kind of not-enough thought. Seeds that can, with practice and persistence, ultimately come to predominately populate your inner being.

The sweet spots that arise from acceptance are analogous to the so-called "zone" that athletes, artists, writers and others who are able to perform or create extraordinary things experience. For them it is the energetic time and space in and from which they can advance to new levels of excellence or creativity. For practitioners of contentment it is the energetic time and space in and from which they can advance to new levels of an appreciative state of mind. Sweet spots are also analogous to the "gap"—the interval between thoughts—which master meditators are said to experience as the entryway to enlightenment or, for some, to God. The receptive internal energy fields activated by acceptance of the arrival of not-enough thinking may not be as numinous as that experienced by master meditators, but they are definitely one in and from which a predominately appreciative state of mind can be cultivated.

There is no substitute for acceptance of our unappreciative more, better, different thoughts. It is simply the one and only antidote to not-enough thinking and the discontentment it evokes.

Reflections

These days I am very clear about the profundity of Carl Jung's statement that "We cannot change anything until we accept it." Having practiced contentment for some time now, I know that accepting the occurrence of unappreciative more, better, different thinking is the only way to lessen the strength of my existing sore spots and avoid the formation of new ones. I also know that it is the only way I can strengthen my existing sweet spots and form new ones.

Looking back on my childhood and adolescent years, I am at a loss to remember or feel the reverberations of any sweet spots. I do not say this to cry "poor me" but just to say that all I can recall or have any perceptible bodily memories of are situations and events which led to the formation of sore spots, not any that hold the life-enriching contentment caused by sweet spots.

I do remember and still frequently feel the echoes of some of the early sweet spots that formed as a result of certain interactions with my first two children. For instance, the awesome sense of serenity I experienced when my first-born infant son fell asleep on my chest after crying out in the middle of the night. The instantaneous and heartfelt satisfaction I experienced with my second-born son as he crawled into my arms one peaceful weekend day. I also remember the sweet spots which formed during my single years when the three of us spent quality time together at my apartment, their sporting events, and on vacation, times in which I would serendipitously relate with one or both of them in ways that left me feeling unreservedly appreciative of our father-son relationship.

I also recall and still frequently feel the reverberations of the many sweet spots that were formed over the course of my now more than thirty-five-year marriage as I became increasingly aware and appreciative of my relationship with my wife. I have come to particularly value how much she truly loves me. I define love as "the giving of time and attention without expecting anything in return," and I know for certain that my wife consistently gives me her time and attention without expecting anything in return. With the appreciation implicit in the practice of contentment, I am increasingly able to effortlessly do the same for her. We have our occasional disagreements and angers with one another, but I truly trust that she really loves me and am immeasurably grateful for the many sweet spots which formed from being in a relationship with her.

I also have a large collection of the sweet spots which formed from my interactions with my two youngest children, who are now adults but were only eight and six respectively at the time of my breakout. I recall the many deeply embedded mind and body memories of times when I was involved with and stood in awe of my daughter: videotaping her as a four- or five-month-old while she meandered around, watching her third-grade dance recital, walking her down the aisle at her wedding. I also fondly recall and feel the warm bodily echoes of the sweet spots which originated from certain interactions with my youngest son: bathing him as an infant, playing chess with him when he was a teenager, observing how he affectionately interacts with his long-standing girlfriend.

My interactions with friends have also resulted in the formation of many sweet spots. This is particularly the case with my men's group friends. During the past twenty years, these are the men with whom I have been able to openly and intimately share the pain of my sore spots and the joy of my sweet spots.

I cherish all of the sweet spots which serendipitously formed from my relationships with my wife, four children and friends. I stunted their strength during my workaholic not-enough thinking years, but since then they seem to serendipitously grow stronger in line with my increasingly frequent appreciative thoughts.

I also cherish some of the sweet spots which formed as a result of my relationship with myself. For example, about five years after my breakout I was just driving along one sunny day and suddenly felt an all-encompassing sense of satisfaction with life and appreciation for everything in and around me. This entirely new experience came out of the blue and only lasted a few seconds, but during that time I was totally at peace with myself and the world, empty of wanting anything more, better or different. It truly was a "peak experience" for me, one that I liken to what the world-renowned late American psychologist, Abraham Maslow, described as "a rare, exciting, oceanic, deeply moving, exhilarating, elevating experience that generates an advanced form of perceiving reality, and is even mystic and magical in its effect."

I imagine that some may find my description of this experience hyperbolic; however, whether it's labeled a peak experience, a zone, a gap, or a sweet spot, this experience was so very new and extraordinary to me that reverberations of it still periodically serve to remind me of the inestimable value of acceptance. Whether acceptance allows us to achieve new levels of excellence or creativity, realize enlightenment, or cultivate contentment, it holds immense power when we realize it. In the language of the practice of contentment, this sweet spot lives on inside me—as most definitely do the ones formed as a result of my relationships with my wife, family and friends. They are all internal fertile fields of energy which not only remain everlastingly available for me to evoke reverberations of the sweetness of life implicit in contentment but also enduringly ripe for me to sow seeds of additional thoughts that are similarly appreciative in nature.

Chapter 11

Acknowledgment

"You can't heal what you don't acknowledge."
Jack Canfield[22]

Acknowledgement is the first of three steps in the mental and emotional journey involved in accreting acceptance of the advent of our not-enough thoughts. It is the inner place from which we must travel to cross over the bridge of surrender, the second step towards acceptance that allows us to forgive the arrival of these kinds of thoughts. Without acknowledgment we wouldn't be able to even set foot on the bridge of surrender. We would be stuck in place, endlessly ensnarled in unceasing circular cycles of not-enough thinking. Until we are able to acknowledge our not-enough thoughts, we will remain unable to make any movement at all towards the third step of acceptance: forgiveness of the occurrences of this type of thinking.

The acknowledgement germane to the practice of contentment is quite different from that involved in most religious practices. The confessional rituals involved in Christianity, Islam and Judaism

---

[22] A contemporary American author and motivational speaker who is best known for his "Chicken Soup for the Soul" series of books which have sold over 500 million copies worldwide.

insinuate some sort of transgression or sin on the part of the acknowledger. Alternatively, the acknowledgement aspired to by practitioners of contentment connotes no such moral error or iniquity.

To acknowledge the arrival of not-enough thinking is to disidentify from it. Silently and serenely saying "hello" to and specifically labeling the occurrence of this type of thinking allows you to engage in the inner act of separating *from* instead of getting lost *in* these thoughts. Acknowledgement involves saying something like the following to yourself: *Hello there my unappreciative more, better, different thought. I am aware that you are a common and normal part of my humanness and want to thank you for the opportunity to notice that I just had another discontent-evoking thought.*

When we acknowledge the arrival of our unappreciative thoughts in this way we can experience them as allies instead of enemies. They become friendly energy forces which provide us with the opportunity to neutralize their discontent-evoking energy and thereby form new or energize our old sweet spots. They become fertile fields of internal energy which are ripe for the infusion of thoughts that are appreciative in nature, catalysts for contentment rather than discontentment.

Acknowledgement allows us to disidentify from our unappreciative more, better, different thoughts so that we can see that any and all of these thoughts are merely ghost-like voices in our heads which would have us believe that we are not-enough or don't have enough: the voice of our childhood self who is still crying out for the attention or affection he or she didn't get; the voices of our parents, teachers and other authority figures who judged, criticized and/or condemned us for not being or doing things more, better and differently; the ubiquitous voices of purveyors of materialism, who persistently tell us that we cannot be content without something or someone that is more, better, or different.

Acknowledgment of the arrival of our not-enough thoughts makes it possible for us to witness them. It allows us to merely observe them without judging, blaming or criticizing ourselves for their occurrence. Acknowledgment creates a calm inner space, like the eye of a hurricane, from which we dispassionately watch any storms of unappreciative thinking that may be whirling around in our heads.

I believe that virtually all of us are capable of acknowledging the advent of our not-enough thoughts. After all, none of our thoughts, including our unappreciative ones, have any inherent power over us whatsoever—unless, that is, we empower them by saying "no" instead of "hello" to their occurrence.

Reflections

I shudder to think about how I was so inexplicably identified with my not-enough thoughts back in my workaholic days. I was so lost in them that I was unable to even acknowledge the occurrence of these kinds of thoughts much less cross over the bridge of surrender that leads to forgiveness of them. Not surprisingly, it took such a calamitous event as my "breakout" for me to begin to undo my enmeshment in them.

It took years of struggle for me to begin to regularly disidentify from the occurrences of my more, better and different thinking around work. It was like letting go of a lover who I knew was wrong for me but on whom I nonetheless continued to fixate.

Eventually my enmeshment with not-enough thinking lessened to the point where I could discern that going back to this former lover would be self-destructive, indeed, masochistic. So upon relocating to Arizona, I realized that any type of work I would do needed to foster a very different way of thinking than that underlying my work addiction. I recognized that I needed to engage in work that would allow me to become increasingly adept at mentally separating *from* instead of getting lost *in* the seductiveness of the not-enough thoughts behind my workaholism.

I knew that returning to a practice of law or the ownership of a business that was primarily aimed at making money would be adverse to this need. I had been there and done that, only to devolve into deeper and deeper depths of discontent and addiction. I considered a career as a mental health professional, but, with my backgrounds in law, business and psychology, I sensed that the role of mediator—someone who helps others resolve conflicts cooperatively and collaboratively— would fit hand-in-glove with my need to disidentify from my not-enough thinking around work. I intuited that helping others resolve their conflicts would also help me resolve mine. This was my chance to clear up the inner conflict between the seductiveness of my not-enough thoughts around work versus my need to acknowledge and, in doing so, disidentify from them.

Now, after many years of practicing mediation as well as contentment, I am very aware that my decision to become a mediator did in fact meet my need to acknowledge my not-enough thoughts around work. It has given me the opportunity to simply and serenely say "hello" to the discontent-producing thoughts behind my workaholism. By helping others acknowledge their not-enough thoughts concerning conflicts in which they were involved, it became clearer and clearer to me that the only way to begin to separate from instead of lose myself in the not-enough thoughts behind my workaholism was to acknowledge them one occurrence at a time. I realized that I needed the disidentification implicit in acknowledgement in order to break free from the recurrent fixations around work that were making it impossible for me to start coming to terms with my not-enough thoughts.

While these fixations have not completely disappeared, they have decreased significantly as I have cultivated increased awareness of the not-enough thinking that evokes them as well as the strength to readily disidentify from the occurrence of this type of thinking. Similarly, although the old sore spots formed by these not-enough thoughts still occasionally become inflamed, I am able to acknowledge their arrival and therefore set myself free to step forward onto the bridge of surrender that leads to forgiveness and facilitates the accretion of acceptance.

Chapter 12

Surrender

*"Be willing to surrender
what you are for what you could become."*
Reinhold Niebuhr[23]

Surrender is the essential second step in the mental and emotional journey towards accreting acceptance of the occurrence of not-enough thinking. It is the inner bridge we must cross over to connect the other two essential aspects of acceptance: our acknowledgment and forgiveness of the occurrence of not-enough thinking.

When we surrender to our not-enough thoughts we are able to yield to and merge with them. Like the Japanese martial art "Aikido" in which a practitioner yields to and merges with the force of aggressive energy so as to redirect it rather than oppose it, a practitioner of contentment endeavors to yield to and merge with the force generated by a not-enough thought.

Surrender denotes non-resistance. It requires an openness rather than opposition to the emergence of not-enough thinking. When we surrender to an incidence of this type of thinking, we demonstrate

---

[23] The 20th century American theologian, ethicist and professor best known for having authored the Serenity Prayer.

an understanding that whatever we resist will persist—regardless of what we do or the lengths we go to in order to repress, suppress, or otherwise resist it.

Once we surrender we also display recognition of our ego's predispositions to misperceive and deny reality. Through this process, we dispel the "illusion of control" as we release our ego's misperception that we can control what someone else thinks, says or does; the outcomes of situations or events; and, relevant to the practice of contentment, the comings and goings of our not-enough thoughts. To be able to surrender we must understand that our ego is predisposed to deny the occurrence of not-enough thinking by completely rejecting it, downplaying its potential to produce negative consequences, or shifting responsibility for it to someone or something else.

Surrender also requires courage and confidence. It reveals the courage implicit in overcoming the commonly held, albeit erroneous, assumption that only the weak or defeated surrender. It also reveals that, like an Aikido master, we have the training, experience and confidence which come from knowing that the extraordinary efficacy of surrender builds the inner bridge needed for us to move from acknowledgement to forgiveness of our not-enough thinking.

Finally, to paraphrase the Serenity Prayer,[24] by surrendering to the occurrences of our not-enough thoughts we will be able to accept the things we cannot change (the occurrence of our not-enough thoughts), have the courage to change the things we can (the negative effects that these kinds of thoughts can have on our feelings and behaviors), and possess the wisdom to know the difference (the difference between surrendering versus opposing the arrival of our not-enough thoughts).

Reflections

My familiarity with surrender began back when I was learning how to dispel the illusion of control which cast a wide net over my thoughts during my workaholic years. In those years I would repeatedly fall prey to this illusion, mistakenly believing that I could actually control clients, colleagues, family and friends by working longer and harder. I mistakenly assumed that if I worked hard enough I could determine how people behaved and how situations and events would turn out, while in actuality I was unwittingly adding fuel to the fire of my addiction.

My breakout provided proof that I don't have this type of control. Like the countless earthquakes I experienced while residing in California, my breakout provided earthshaking evidence of the gross misperception of the mind I accepted when I believed that we can control anything at all, except

---

[24] "God, grant me the serenity to accept the things I cannot change, the courage to change the things I can, and wisdom to know the difference."

perhaps our own behavior. Additionally, my breakout facilitated my understanding of the importance of surrendering to the arrival of my not-enough thoughts. It primed the pump for me to begin yielding to and merging with the energy generated by these kinds of thoughts—thereby hastening the healing of my sore spots.

My breakout also eased my escape from denial of the occurrence of unappreciative thinking. Before this time I was a proud workaholic, completely rejecting any notion that my behavior was adversely affecting my life. After this awakening, it was virtually impossible for me to downplay or otherwise deny the negative impacts of my obsessive behavior along with the not-enough thinking from which it originated.

The Serenity Prayer was one of the first things I learned at the treatment center for workaholism. For the first few weeks I was so deeply despondent that I clung to this prayer like a life preserver, silently saying it over and over and over again to scarcely stay afloat in relentlessly stormy seas of severe anxiety and fear. Now, many years later, this prayer still provides me with the mental and emotional wherewithal I need to merge with and yield to the occurrence of some of my more anxiety-arousing and fear-facilitating unappreciative thoughts. Comparable to the *Sweet Surrender* that the late songwriter and actor John Denver wrote about, I can now weather any sort of stormy sea that may have been roiled by the occurrence of not-enough thinking like "a fish in the water" and "a bird in the air" by surrendering to the occurrence of these types of thoughts.

Chapter 13

Forgiveness

*"Forgiveness says that you are giving
another chance to make a new beginning."*
Desmond Tutu[25]

Forgiveness, the act of pardoning ourselves or someone else for a mistake or wrongdoing, is the third essential step in the mental and emotional journey towards accreted acceptance. It is the voluntary action of choosing absolution over anger; amends over aversion. For practitioners of contentment, it is the act of forgiving the incidence of unappreciative more, better, different thinking.

Many religious faiths, spiritual groups, and self-help programs encourage us to ask ourselves as well as others for forgiveness. These traditions recognize that the very act of asking for forgiveness functions to release the guilt and perhaps even shame we feel from something that in retrospect we genuinely regret.

When we forgive the arrival of not-enough thinking we can begin to detach from it.

---

[25] A contemporary South African retired Anglican Bishop and social rights advocate.

Forgiveness involves the inner act of disengaging from the emotions evoked by the occurrence of our unappreciative thoughts which allows us to see that any and all degrees of discontent are just bodily reactions to our not-enough thoughts: the mad, bad, sad feelings and the fears and desires which are the predictable and often painful products of not-enough thinking and our attachment to it.

To forgive is not the same as to forget. As the 19th Century renowned philosopher, George Santayana, said, "Those who do not learn from history are doomed to repeat it." If we forget the history of the unappreciative discontent we experienced as a result of our not-enough thoughts, we are doomed to continuously repeat the varying degrees of dissatisfaction and dissonance they generated. Absent awareness, we also waste valuable lessons from our past. We may miss the opportunity to see that each experience of discontent, no matter how deep, is ultimately for our good. Without experiences of struggle and discontent, we may never come to realize the need to practice contentment and reap the goodness that comes from this journey. To forgive the occurrence of an unappreciative thought is a decision to pardon rather than punish ourselves for having had or actually acted upon a not-enough thought. In the words of Bishop Tutu, when we forgive we give ourselves "the chance to make a new beginning." In the context of the practice of contentment, this new beginning means the chance to cultivate sweet spots instead of sore spots.

Reflections

Looking back I can see that I first experienced the power of forgiveness as a result of working through the stages central to all 12-Steps recovery programs. In accordance with Step 8, I "made a list of all persons... [I had] harmed and became willing to make amends to them," including myself. In accordance with Step 9, I "made direct amends to such people wherever possible...." Later on, I also experienced the power of forgiveness when I asked forgiveness of any harm I had done to myself and others in the preceding year in observation of the Jewish New Year.

These days, I am well aware of the power of forgiveness when practicing contentment. Knowing that repeated incidences of unappreciative thinking are inevitable, I endeavor to forgive rather than condemn myself for their occurrence. After all, to do otherwise would be to imprison myself in myriad degrees and dimensions of discontent—as did one holocaust survivor who inquired of another survivor decades after his release from a Nazi concentration camp: "Are you still angry about being imprisoned in the camp?" The second survivor replied: "Damn right I am; I will never forgive those bastards!" To which the first survivor said with sadness: "So, my friend, it seems that you are still imprisoned." Clearly our not-enough thoughts and unappreciative beliefs can be strong prisons if we give them the power to keep a grasp on us by failing to engage in forgiveness.

Of note, although not directly relevant to forgiveness, I want to point out that the Nazi concentration camps were a prime example of the dehumanization and debasement that can ensue from extreme not-enough thinking. After all, the Nazi's believed that they were superiorly more, better, different than everyone else, which they used in an attempt to justify their murdering of millions of people.

When repeatedly practiced, the inner processes involved in forgiveness function, in conjunction with those involved in acknowledgement and surrender, to incrementally increase the size and strength of our sweet spots. In other words, they accrete acceptance.

Chapter 14

Accreted Acceptance

"Accept things as they are, and look realistically at the world around you. Have faith in yourself and in the direction you have chosen."
Ralph Marston[26]

Acknowledgement, surrender and forgiveness allow us to progress on the journey towards accreted acceptance of our not-enough thoughts. With repeated recognition of the occurrences of our not-enough thoughts, we accrete acceptance of them. In other words, each time we engage in acknowledging, surrendering to, and forgiving the arrival of these kinds of thoughts, we build acceptance.

The process of acceptance is nonlinear, nondualistic and unpredictable. Acceptance accretes like a rollercoaster, in a nonlinear up and down and all round fashion. For instance, in one moment we may be building up an increasingly greater capacity to readily go through all of the aspects of acceptance but in the very next we may find ourselves opposing rather than surrendering to it.

---

[26] An early 20th Century professional football player.

The accretion of acceptance also proceeds nondualistically. There are many shades of gray between the black and white dualism of readily acknowledging that a not-enough thought has occurred and resolutely refusing to forgive it— with any shade, no matter how light or dark, producing at least some semblance of acceptance. Therefore, even just a little bit of acknowledgment combined with a dash of forgiveness will give rise to at least some semblance of acceptance.

Acceptance also accretes in nonscheduled ways. There is simply no way to predict at what point in the processes involved in acceptance that we will come to terms with the occurrence of a particular not-enough thought. Whereas a touch of acknowledgement alone may be all that we need to accept the arrival of some of our relatively benign not-enough thoughts, it may require a big buildup of all of the aspects of acceptance for us to come to grips with some really reprehensible ones. There is also no telling how long it will take for our acceptance of the advent of a not-enough thought to accrete. It might happen quite quickly, such as when we instantly go from acknowledgement to forgiveness of its incidence. On the other hand, it might progress slowly as occurs when the discontent derived from a not-enough thought is so deeply embedded in our psyche and our bodily reactions to it are so particularly painful, that it takes years to fully accrete all of the aspects of acceptance.

In light of its nonlinear, nondualistic and nonscheduled nature, the accretion of acceptance of some of our really reprehensible not-enough thoughts may seem daunting if not impossible. But we can take heart in knowing that each time we acknowledge, surrender to, and/or forgive the occurrence of the same or similar not-enough thought, our capacity to further accrete acceptance of it will increase in potency and power. Like the automatic increase in the value of an interest-bearing bank account, our capacity for acceptance of the arrival of unappreciative thinking will automatically grow greater each time we employ any of its aspects.

Just as recovering alcoholics, workaholics and other addicts must constantly strive to accept the vicissitudes of life "one day at a time," a practitioner of contentment must aspire to accept one not-enough thought at a time. As Ralph Marston said, you must repeatedly do your best to "have faith in yourself and in the direction you have chosen."

Reflections

Even with all my years of practicing contentment and my knowledge about the components of acceptance, it's still sometimes difficult to build up even a small amount of acceptance of my particularly painful not-enough thought patterns. For example, when a recurrent not-enough thought relates to my wife or children, I may feel such great guilt or even shame over having had it that it's often challenging to build up any amount of acceptance of it. Instead, I completely lose sight of the reality that the occurrence of these kinds of thoughts doesn't mean that I am bad, mean, or anything like that. When I am amidst such painful thought patterns, I can no longer see that these kinds of thoughts are delusional, fantastical and fictional and that they will continually cross my mind no matter how accomplished I am in practicing contentment.

I also sometimes find myself rushing right past one or more components of acceptance and into immediately taking some sort of action when I am entwined in these particularly painful not-enough thought patterns. For example, when I fall prey to the combined effects of delusional not-enough thinking and the illusion of control, I am apt to skip over the acknowledgement, surrender and forgiveness requisite to acceptance and, instead, rush right into taking action regardless of the negative consequences. Intellectually I realize that rushing past acceptance directly into action never works. I know that acceptance is indeed the one and only antidote to not-enough thinking, but sometimes the combined effects of these confusions of my mind make me imprudently impatient to take any time at all to accrete acceptance.

I know from my experiences that it can be frustrating if not infuriating to repeatedly have to build up acceptance of some of our recurrent not-enough thoughts, especially those that we deem abhorrent. But I have also discovered that virtually every one of us can accrete acceptance of even the vilest of our recurrent not-enough thoughts with patience, persistence and perseverance. Much like "catch-and-release" fishing, all we need do to accrete acceptance is *catch* each occurrence of this type of thinking with awareness and *release* it with acknowledgment, surrender and forgiveness.

Part Three
ACTION

"Accept—then Act."
Eckhart Tolle

Chapter 15

The Efficacy of Action

"My mind is a garden. My thoughts are the seeds.
My harvest will be either flowers or weeds."
Mel Weldon[27]

Practitioners of contentment aspire to engage in those types of actions which will strengthen the efficacy of their sweet spots to evoke contentment. They do their best to sow seeds of appreciative thoughts in the fertile fields of neutralized inner energy which formed or expanded each time they became aware of and accepted the occurrence of unappreciative more, better, different thinking. By taking these kinds of actions, including those described in the following chapters, practitioners "harvest flowers rather than weeds."

All of the actions which empower our sweet spots to generate contentment require "mindfulness." In general terms, mindfulness is "the intentional, accepting and non-judgmental focus of one's attention on the emotions, thoughts and sensations occurring in the present moment."[28] Specific to the practice of contentment,

---

[27] An influential 19th-20th Century Christian Minister.
[28] https://en.wikipedia.org/wiki/Mindfulness

mindfulness involves purposefully paying attention to the occurrences of our not-enough thoughts as well as the diverse degrees of discontent they cause. Like a microscope, mindful awareness of the arrival of our not-enough thoughts brings clarity to what we could not otherwise see. It brings into focus the reality that in the absence of awareness and acceptance these kinds of thoughts inevitably produce a host of negative emotional and behavioral consequences.

All of the actions which increase the effectiveness of our sweet spots also require patience and persistence. None of them are a one-and-done fix. On the contrary, a practitioner of contentment must continually engage in such actions due to the ubiquity of not-enough conditioning which requires persistent awareness and mindfulness to overcome.

The actions described in the following chapters are not intended as an exhaustive list. They are only the ones that have proven effective in my practice of contentment. It's as likely as not that others of equal efficacy will become evident in the course of time.

Reflections

The longer I practice contentment, the greater my commitment becomes to regularly take those actions which increase the efficacy of my sweet spots. This practice and the sweet spots it has given rise to have changed my life in so many wonderful ways. I would be crazy to not only continue taking these actions but to add new ones as well.

I was initially introduced to the concept of "mindfulness" by my first Workaholics Anonymous Sponsor, who would occasionally caution me, "*Don't go in your head alone, Oliver. It's a dangerous place to be.*" He didn't label it as mindfulness, but I now realize that this caution was meant to encourage me to be mindful of my thoughts so as to avoid their potentially "dangerous" consequences.

My purposeful practice of mindfulness began back when I was investigating the connection between unmet expectations and unhappiness (Chapter 3). Although I didn't identify it as a mindfulness practice at the time, that's exactly what I was doing. Each time I intentionally became aware of the fact that my unhappiness was derived from my own unfulfilled expectant thinking, I was purposefully practicing mindfulness.

In the years following this investigation, I experimented with different methods of mindfulness. For varying lengths of time I engaged in several different approaches to meditation. All of these techniques, including the approach I currently practice, were in one way or another directed towards increasing my capacity to purposefully pay attention to my thoughts and feelings. I also participated in a few mindfulness-oriented groups and trainings, including one based in the secular system of mindfulness developed by the renowned contemporary molecular biologist and professor, Jon Kabat-Zinn.[29]

As I have built my awareness and ability to recognize my thoughts through these practices and experiences, I am far less likely to significantly suffer any of the negative emotional and behavioral consequences which commonly follow not-enough thinking. I am no longer prone to sink to the depths of anger and sadness, or the extreme extents of fear and desire, as I did before. I am also much less apt to reflexively react, widen the cracks in my relationships, contract "affluenza," become addicted to a substance or behavior, or develop one of the countless sicknesses consequential to the stress of mindlessly seeking endless more, better, or different things instead of appreciating what I already have.

The ability of my sweet spots to generate greater and longer lasting moments of contentment is truly awesome! Yet the efficacy of taking the actions described in the following chapters doesn't end there. Along with the contentment generated by my sweet spots, my capacity for compassion, empathy and humility has markedly increased as I have cultivated mindfulness.

---

[29] A Professor of Medicine at the University of Massachusetts Medical School who began a Mindfulness-Based Stress Reduction (MBSR) program which since then has been adopted by numerous other institutions including hospitals, schools and prisons in many different countries.

Before I appreciated the power of practicing contentment and taking action to purposefully cultivate my sweet spots, I was self-centeredly focused on getting and achieving more, better and different things. However, these days I typically respond to someone else's suffering in kind and caring ways. My capacity for empathy has increased in tandem with taking the actions involved in nurturing my sweet spots. Nowadays I usually try to understand and otherwise walk in the shoes of someone who appears to be having a difficult time. Whereas in the past, especially during my workaholic years, I was often arrogant and oblivious of any damage done by what I said or did to friends, business colleagues and even some family members, these days I greatly value my overall humbleness.

The practice of contentment is a specialized method of mindfulness. It is a particular protocol for purposefully paying attention to the occurrence of not-enough thinking and the discontent it inevitably evokes in the absence of awareness and acceptance. With mindfulness, we can infuse our existing sweet spots with thoughts that are appreciative in nature and form new ones, each time incrementally increasing our natural wealth of contentment.

Chapter 16

Re-Parent Yourself

"The child within sees us as the parent."
Michael Brown[30]

You re-parent yourself by decreasing the volume of the parental voices in your head while simultaneously increasing the volume of your adult voice. These "parental voices" include those of your parents, teachers and other so-called authority figures which keep telling your child within that he or she should have been or currently could be more, better, and/or different. This "adult voice" is the one that speaks for your mature self. It represents that grownup part of you that is fully aware of the falsity of these parental voices and thus completely capable of diminishing the sensitivity of your sore spots while simultaneously strengthening the efficacy of your sweet ones.

The groundbreaking work of Dr. Eric Berne[31] is right on point with regards to this concept. Dr. Berne's model of "Transactional Analysis" suggests

---

[30] A contemporary author and speaker who created a paradigm for heightened consciousness known as "The Presence Process."

[31] A 20th Century psychiatrist who created a highly effective theoretical basis for and therapeutic approach to personal development, and the author of the best-selling book, "Games People Play".

that although we interact with others from three distinct ego states—child, adult, and parent—very few of us are aware of which one of these states is operative at any given time. This work also posits that our personal development is dependent on the extent to which we can wield the authority of our adult ego state when interacting with our child ego state.

For Berne, these three ego states are present in each of us and can be confirmed with observable behaviors. The child ego state appears in the form of two internal voices: the "natural" child who freely and spontaneously interacts with others; and the "adapted" child who constantly adjusts his or her interactions to those perceived as likely to please others. The "parent" ego state shows up as the ingrained and often castigating voices of the people who shaped our values, beliefs and personality. The voice of our grownup self is expressed via the "adult" ego state which demonstrates the knowledge and experience required to protect and otherwise take care of the child self.

Berne's Transactional Analyses can be applied to the re-parenting involved in the practice of contentment. Using this model, we see that we must assert our adult ego state whenever we become aware that our adapted child is distressed or otherwise discontent. Each time our adapted child cries out for more, better and/or different attention or affection, we must assert our adult voice to assure him (or her) that we are fully capable of assuaging any degree of discontent he is experiencing as a result of one of his sore spots having been inflamed. We must let him know that we are knowledgeable about the origins and nature of his not-enough thoughts as well as the acceptance required to activate sweet spots instead of inflame sore ones. Further, we need to confirm that we are adept at filling these sweet spots with appreciative thoughts which bring forth contentment rather than discontentment.

By re-parenting yourself in this way, your adapted child "sees you as the parent" whom is ready, willing and able to dampen the discontent emanating from your sore spots. Each time you re-parent yourself in this way, your adapted child grows increasingly confident that your adult-self is equipped to not only diminish the intensity of your sore spots but to also heighten the contentment-evoking efficacy of your sweet spots.

Reflections

Re-parenting—being aware of and interacting as an adult with my adapted child—resoundingly reduced the sensitivity of two of my particularly sensitive sore spots. It dramatically dampened the volume of the parental voices which continually told me that I was not worth enough nor smart enough to deserve their attention or affection, much less their love.

Both of these sore spots originated when I was in elementary school. The first formed from the abandonments I experienced as a result of both of my parents' extreme emotional unavailability. Like any young child, I internalized these experiences. I subconsciously convinced myself that "*I am not worthy enough to warrant their attention and affection*"—and thereafter unconsciously feared abandonment in all of my other relationships.

The second of these sore spots formed from the sometimes explicit and other times implied "*you are stupid*" messages which I received as a child and adolescent from my parents, one of my grandparents, and two of my schoolteachers. Despite all of my subsequent educational and career achievements, the belief that I was indeed stupid subconsciously persisted. This created an extremely sensitive sore spot which led me to become instantly enraged whenever I perceived that someone had labeled me as not smart enough.

Needless to say, these sore spots were the source of countless discontentments and disruptions. Like an invisible rope around my neck, they yanked me from one discontentment to another and led to many disruptive if not destructive behaviors.

It wasn't until several years after my breakout that I was able to begin to dispel both of these not-enough beliefs and lessen the sensitivity of the sore spots they had formed. I was able to apply everything I was learning about myself, including how to interact as an adult with my adapted child, to re-parent myself and thus break free of most of the discontentments and disruptions that had previously beset me.

Now, having practiced contentment for many years, my ability to re-parent myself has developed to new and immensely important heights. For example, when my wife and I went through a rough patch in our relationship, I was able to repeatedly assert my adult-self to sooth the sore spots created by my adapted child's abandonment experiences. Instead of the abject anxiety that formerly consumed me when my wife and I were seriously at odds, my adult-self was able to demonstrably defuse the intensity of these sore spots. By re-parenting myself, I shifted from reactionary behavior to considered action. Instead of falling prey to the fear-based reflexive reactions that would have theretofore ensued and exacerbated the situation, I cleared the way for contentment and the relationship-enhancing actions that stem from it.

With the re-parenting involved in the practice of contentment, I now have the knowledge about and experience with the occurrence of not-enough thinking to assure my adapted child that he is worthy enough, smart enough, and in all other respects *enough*. Irrespective of the circumstances at hand, I am confident that my adult-self is resolutely ready, willing and able to responsibly respond rather than reflexively react to the inflammation of any kind of sore spot, thereby enhancing the efficacy of my sweet spots and further enriching my natural wealth of contentment.

Chapter 17

Unwind Yourself from Worry

*"If only the people who worry about
their liabilities would think about the riches
they do possess, they would stop worrying."*
Dale Carnegie[32]

Worry is a particularly prevalent form of unappreciative more, better, different thinking. Virtually all of us periodically conjure up more, better, and different *what if* and *if only* not-enough worrisome thoughts. Worry floods our minds with thoughts like *"What if I could've done this or that more, better or differently?"* and *"If only I could do such and such more, better, or differently... "*

Like a boa constrictor, worry relentlessly tightens its grip on you. It wickedly winds its way around your mind, sapping the strength of your sweet spots and constricting your thoughts to mostly unappreciative ones. As it incites unappreciative thinking, worry evokes increasingly deeper despair, dread and other forms of discontent, inflaming your sore spots while precluding any plausible possibility of contentment.

---

[32] The 20th Century American writer and lecturer who developed widely acclaimed courses in self-improvement, salesmanship, public speaking and interpersonal skills.

Intellectually you know that it's futile to worry. You understand that no matter how hard or long you worry, it will only hinder rather than help your ability to be aware of and accept this form of not-enough thinking. Nevertheless, nearly all of us allow the mind to manufacture an almost constant stream of not-enough worrisome thoughts. Time and again we will worry about getting or not losing an endless variety of more, better or different things, only to lose sleep and concentration. Over time this persistent unease excludes the calmness of contentment.

For all of these reasons, practitioners of contentment must do their best to disentangle themselves from the occurrence of not-enough worrisome thoughts. Instead of allowing worry to tighten its grip and constrict their thoughts to those focused on what they don't have or may lose, practitioners strive to appreciate what they do have. They are able to emphasize the "riches" they already possess instead of worrying about their "liabilities" and can thereby strengthen the efficacy of their sweet spots to engender contentment.

Reflections

As you may recall, there was a time when my mind ran so rampant with worrisome thoughts that I was persistently plagued with anxiety, dread and other degrees of discontent (Chapter 2). There was also a time when the only way I could fall asleep at night was to intentionally think of something about which to worry (Chapter 8).

The first time I actually began to focus on my worrisome thoughts was during my in-patient treatment for workaholism. There was a poster on the wall in one of the common rooms that proclaimed, "WORRY IS AN INSULT TO GOD." It didn't take long for me to understand that worry is a subset of fear, and that as such it cannot co-exist with faith. I realized that faith and fear (including its subset, worry) are mutually exclusive, and from then on did my best not to insult God—albeit far from flawlessly.

After treatment, my focus on worrisome thoughts sharpened as I gradually became used to certain 12-Steps practices. Once again the Serenity Prayer served me well, this time diminishing the dread generated by these kinds of thoughts. So did practicing the "Three C's": "You didn't cause it. You can't control it. You can't cure it." I did my best to prevent worry from winding around and constricting my mind by remembering that I didn't cause the occurrence of these types of not-enough thoughts; that their occurrence is a natural product of the way my brain is structured and how I was conditioned to think. I also reminded myself that although I can influence such thoughts, I cannot control how they affect my emotions and behaviors. Further, I realized that I can't cure nor entirely eliminate worrisome thoughts.

In addition to the foregoing 12-Steps practices, these days I regularly rely on the following reality check to unwind myself from the occurrence of not-enough worrisome thoughts. First I silently ask myself if there is anything I can do right now to influence or change the situation I want to be more, better, and/or different. If the answer is "yes," I do it. For instance, a while ago I started to worry about a serious situation involving one of my adult sons. Instead of letting it wind its way around my mind and continuing to lose sleep, I asked myself if there was anything I could do or say at that very moment to influence or change his situation. And because the answer was affirmative, I got out of bed and telephoned him just to say hello and that I love him. If, however, the answer to this question is "no," I proceed to recall the reality that worry doesn't do any good whatsoever—for me or for the person I am worried about. This reminder is usually all I need to unwind myself from these particularly prevalent and pernicious types of not-enough thoughts.

Chapter 18

Remind Yourself

*"Men more frequently require
to be reminded than informed."*
Samuel Johnson[33]

Reminders play a part in most of our everyday lives. We set an alarm clock to remind us when we want to wake up in the morning. We book appointments in our calendars to remind us with whom, when and where we are scheduled to meet. We write shopping lists to remind us what we need to buy. These are but a few of the ways in which we use reminders to remember things.

In addition to these everyday uses, practitioners of contentment utilize reminders to prompt the production of appreciative thoughts. Knowing that thoughts based in appreciation are catalysts for contentment, practitioners use a variety of reminders to energize their existing sweet spots as well as activate new ones.

One way that you can promote the production of appreciative thoughts is to periodically prepare a list of the people and circumstances in your life for whom and about which you are grateful. This is commonly known as a "gratitude list." When done

---

[33] An 18th century English prominent essayist and literary historian.

consistently, this exercise will remind you to appreciate what you already have, or in other words, to count your blessings.

Another way to use reminders to prompt appreciative thoughts is to write down one or more meaningful words on a piece of paper and place it where you will see it regularly—around your house, office or any other place you frequent. Just as traffic signals prompt you to remember rules of the road, a written note which contains words relating to the practice of contentment will prompt you to remember to be appreciative.

The cultivation of certain ritualistic behaviors will also promote the production of appreciative thoughts. For example, when beginning to fall asleep, you can make a habit of mentally reminding yourself about those things in your day that you appreciate. You can also recurrently read or listen to some sort of self-help, spiritual or other personal growth books or audio recordings, any of which is likely to directly or indirectly remind you to be appreciative.

All of the foregoing reminders are actions you can take to repeatedly remember the efficacy of infusing your sweet spots with thoughts that are appreciative in nature. As you engage in these habits you will undoubtedly develop the attitude of gratitude that is characteristic of contentment.

Reflections

Early on in my recovery from workaholism I learned about the benefits of regularly composing a gratitude list. For as Melody Beatte, the author of the bestselling book, *Codependent No More*, said, "Gratitude turns what we have into enough, and more. It turns denial into acceptance, chaos into order, confusion into clarity...it makes sense of our past, brings peace for today, and creates a vision for tomorrow."

These days I am acutely aware of the efficacy of gratitude when developing the attitude of appreciation instrumental to practicing contentment. So, when beginning to fall asleep each evening, I mentally compose a list of all of my actions and interactions from that day about which I am particularly appreciative. Similarly, upon arising each morning, I prompt the production of appreciative thoughts by reading a page or two of an inspirational book.

Written reminders also play an important part in prompting my appreciative thinking. For example, when first starting to practice contentment I put a yellow Post-it® note with the letters "MBD" on the inside fold of my wallet to signify the initial letters in the words *More*, *Better*, and *Different*. Whenever I opened it, these letters would prompt my awareness of the delusion implicit in this type of thinking. Later on, I replaced this note with one on which I had written the letters "UMBD," which served to regularly remind me about the *unappreciative* nature of more, better, different thinking. These days, the Post-it® note in my wallet has the word "APPRECIATION" written on it, repeatedly reminding me of the serenity that accrues from the attitude of gratitude engendered by practicing contentment.

I also have the same or similarly written Post-it® notes strategically placed in several different locations in my home, office and car. For example, I recently put one on the dashboard of my car to continually remind me to appreciate the beauty of nature—the trees, the mountains, the sky and all of its many other splendors—as I drive along.

All of these reminders hold me in good stead as I continue to progress in the practice of contentment. Each night when I am beginning to fall asleep, the mental list I make of the people and circumstances about which I am grateful prompts my rekindled appreciation for my relationship with my wife and other loved ones. Further, it reminds me of those things which I already have and achieved which renews my appreciation for them. Each morning when I am reading something inspirational, the ensuing thought processes remind me to be appreciative of the great extent to which the practice of contentment is so closely aligned with personal inner growth.

Day in and day out these reminders periodically promote thoughts based in gratitude for my having become knowledgeable about the whys and wherefores of not-enough thinking as well as the negative emotional and behavioral consequences which would ensue if I didn't have this knowledge. In short, all of these reminders go a long way "to turn what... [I] have into enough."

Chapter 19

Center Yourself

*"At the center of your being you have the answer;
you know who you are and you know what you
want."*
Lao Tzu[34]

In general terms, when you center yourself you consciously connect to your mind and emotions. Like an anchor prevents a ship from running aground, centering yourself prevents your thoughts and feelings from running aground in the unalterable past or imagined future. Instead when you are centered, your thoughts remain grounded in the actual reality of the present moment.

In the practice of contentment, centering yourself is the act of consciously connecting to the sweet spots which formed as you became aware of and accepted the advent of an unappreciative more, better, different thought. It is a way to "know who you are and... what you want." When you are centered, you are empowered to choose to accrue the benefits of practicing contentment instead of continuing to fall prey to the negative emotional

---

[34] An ancient Chinese philosopher and founder of Taoism (which advocates humility and religious piety as pathways to the divine).

and behavioral consequences of not-enough thinking.

There are a variety of strategies for centering yourself when practicing contentment. Primary among these are conscious breathing, purposeful praying, and regular meditation.

Consciously breathing to center oneself is one of the most accessible as well as most powerful ways that we can seed our sweet spots with appreciative thoughts. This technique is readily accessible, allowing us to utilize it wherever we are no matter what we are doing. The breath is with you at all times, day or night. It's powerful because it unites whatever degree of discontent physically manifests with the unappreciative thought that preceded it. For these reasons, the breath is recognized in many traditions as "vital energy," "breath of life," "spirit," "chi" (the Chinese word for energy flow), and "prana" (the Hindu word for life force). Likewise, Thich Nhat Hanh, the prominent contemporary Vietnamese Zen Buddhist monk, teacher, author, poet, and peace activist, said, "Breath is the bridge which connects life to consciousness, which unites your body to your thoughts."

Unfortunately, most of us pay little if any attention to our breath. The autonomic nervous system functions independently of our conscious control to regulate our breath as well as our heartbeat and several other bodily functions. Due to the automatic nature of this system, most of us don't pay any attention to even a few of the thousands of breaths we take each day. It's also unfortunate that most of us are apt to momentarily hold our breath when we feel anxious, stressed or similarly discontent. By holding it in we prevent rather than promote its power to become a "bridge" between the discontent we are experiencing and the not-enough thought that precipitated it.

When practicing contentment, consciously breathing to center yourself allows you to promote rather than prevent the expansion of your sweet spots. The ease of access and power of the breath makes it an always available means to increase the efficacy of the energy within our sweet spots, thereby generating many moments of contentment.

Praying is another way to purposely center yourself in your sweet spots. Because appreciation has been characterized as the highest form of prayer,[35] it makes sense that centering yourself by engaging in the act of praying will increase your awareness and acceptance of the occurrence of not-enough thinking and evoke contentment.

It doesn't matter whether you pray to the God of the Hebrew or Christian Bibles, Allah, Krishna, a prophet, a saint, or any other God of your understanding. After all, centering ourselves in our internal energy spots which are devoid of

---

[35] "Appreciation is the highest form of prayer, for it acknowledges the presence of good wherever you shine the light of your thankful thoughts." Alan Cohen, an extremely successful and highly regarded American businessman.

unappreciative more, better, different thinking (i.e., our sweet spots), might be as close as any of us can come to ascending to heaven on earth.

Meditation—the act of directing your attention in a careful and considered way—is yet another highly effective means of centering yourself. In the practice of contentment, it is the act of deliberately directing your attention to thoughts which are appreciative in nature. This focused attention allows you to activate new or invigorate your existing sweet spots.

There are quite a few different meditation methods and means which will center us in our sweet spots when regularly employed. For example, you can focus your attention on those things that you appreciate about yourself, your family and friends, and your life circumstances. These techniques can be done while sitting, standing, reclining, walking, driving, or doing virtually anything else that is conducive to becoming increasingly aware of the whys and wherefores of your unappreciative thinking, the efficacy of accepting this type of thinking, and the actions you can take to activate new and increase the contentment-generating ability of your existing sweet spots.

It's not necessary to meditate for hours at a time. In my experience, doing so for as little as ten minutes each day is likely to advance the infusion of appreciative thoughts in our sweet spots. Nor is it necessary to become a Buddhist, follow any other religious faith or spiritual tradition, or employ any specific technique. As Jon Kabat-Zinn[36] said in regards to his book, *Wherever You Go, There You Are: Mindfulness Meditation in Everyday Life*, "It's not about Buddhism, but about paying attention. That's what all meditation is, no matter what tradition or particular technique is used."

Apropos to the practice of contentment, meditation is about "paying attention" to the occurrences of your unappreciative more, better, different thoughts. It is the act of directing your attention to the arrival of these types of thoughts in order to strengthen the efficacy of your sweet spots to generate the satisfaction and serenity concomitant to contentment—"no matter what tradition or particular technique is used."

Finally, it's important to note that all three of the foregoing methods and means of activating new and enriching our existing sweet spots can be used in combination with or separately from several other ways of doing so. Specific to the practice on contentment, these other methods and means include *affirmations* (i.e., the act of proclaiming your intent to steadfastly seed your mind with appreciative thoughts), *vows* (i.e., the act of pledging to persistently seed your mind with appreciative thoughts), and *visualizations* (i.e., the act of forming mental images of how your life would look if your mind were to be predominately populated with appreciative thoughts).

---

[36] *Ibid* Chapter 15, footnote 22

Reflections

I became aware of some of the benefits which accrue from consciously breathing long before I began to develop the practice of contentment. For example, even at the height of my workaholism, I knew that consciously breathing while jogging would bring forth the benefits of mental quietude and physical relaxation. Indeed, I would wager that it was the echoes of these benefits that subconsciously provided the impetus for me to first become aware of the connection between my expectant thoughts and unhappiness (Chapter 3) and, years later, the origins, nature and consequences of not-enough thinking (Chapters 5-9).

These days I consciously utilize my breath to activate new and bolster my existing sweet spots in countless different settings. For instance, when I am in the midst of exercising and a not-enough thought pops into my head, such as *I could be doing something else that's more, better or different*, I intentionally breathe so as to center myself in appreciation for the very fact that I am physically fit enough to workout. Similarly, while I am mediating a dispute and I can't think of anything to say or do to facilitate agreement, I consciously employ my breath to center myself in the calmness of my sweet spots, trusting that what is best to say or do will spontaneously surface usually much sooner than later. Another time when I employ the power of conscious breathing is when I am involved in some everyday activity and a not-enough thought arises to the effect that I am not enough in this or that respect. In this situation,

I consciously breathe to center myself in appreciation for my positive attributes and accomplishments.

All in all I strive to do my best to consciously breathe as much as possible such that my mind produces appreciative as opposed to unappreciative thoughts. For as Eckhart Tolle said in his bestselling book, *A New Earth,*[37] "Being aware of your breath forces you into the present moment—the key to all inner transformation. Whenever you are conscious of the breath, you are absolutely present. You cannot think and be aware of your breathing. Conscious breathing stops your mind... Be aware of your breathing as often as you are able, whenever you remember. Do that for one year, and it will be... powerfully transformative."

I have also discovered the power of prayer as I have grown in my practice of contentment. Prayer was the farthest thing from my mind before my breakout. Despite having been raised as a Jew, albeit on a surface level, before this breakout there was little if anything I knew about praying, much less how to do it. In fact, from adolescence to my late forties I didn't know anything about prayer.

Of course, my attitude towards prayer dramatically changed as a result of my breakout. It was then that the Serenity Prayer became "powerfully transformative" for me. It became and continues to be one of the very effective ways by

---

[37] A New Earth: Awakening to Your Life's Purpose, (2005) Penguin Publications.

which I purposely center myself so as to release the contentment-generating energy stored in my sweet spots.

In the same way, mediation has become an essential part of my daily life. Like taking certain medications or brushing my teeth, I am convinced that setting aside time to meditate each day is not only good for physical health but also for my mental, emotional and spiritual health.

Even back in my workaholic years I periodically dabbled in meditation. I don't remember the details of how or why I sometimes meditated, but I do recall using some kind of mantra, a word or phrase that I repeated over and over again, to try to focus my attention on something other than work. I also remember taking a ten session meditation course at a local university.

When we relocated from Los Angeles to Phoenix a few years after my breakout, I became involved in a nondenominational spiritual group which emphasized meditation. I also started reading literature about meditation and began to actually practice it each morning as part of a prayer ritual—which, as things turned out, was the method of meditation I employed for the next decade or so. This daily routine definitely deepened my attraction to meditation and no doubt led to my currently abiding practice of a Buddhist variation of it.

These days my current morning meditation practice incorporates conscious breathing, a prayer for compassion, and a mediation on appreciation. I usually sit for twenty minutes, and this practice typically unfolds in the following fashion.

I consciously use my breath to center myself from beginning to end. Having experienced my breath as a powerful agent for activating awareness for many years now, it is an essential part of my morning mediation.

After a minute or so of consciously breathing, I silently say my version of a prayer that Jack Kornfield included in his book, *The Wise Heart*.[38] Basically, I substitute the word contentment for the word compassion as follows: "May you be held in contentment. May the pain and sorrow from your not-enough thoughts be eased. May you be at peace in predominately appreciative thoughts." [And,] "May I be held in contentment. May the pain and sorrow of my not-enough thoughts be eased. May I be at peace in predominately appreciative thoughts." During this time I visualize any of my loved ones close friends or anyone else who is particularly discontent and pray that he or she will be held in contentment. I also visualize my own dimensions of discontent and pray that my pain and sorrow may be eased.

Next, I meditate on the word "appreciation." On my in-breath I bring to mind the first syllable of this word (i.e., "ap") and on my out-breath the last four (i.e., "pre-ci-a-tion"). It is in this way that I

---

[38] The Wise Heart: A Guide to the Universal Teaching of Buddhist Psychology, (2009) Bantam Books.

consciously evoke the soothing sense of satisfaction and serenity stored in my sweet spots.

I strongly encourage you to give this method of meditation a try because it has indeed proven to be an extremely effective method of exponentially expanding the energy of our sweet spots and thus generating much greater contentment. And, you don't have to sitting for twenty minutes or have your eyes closed to garner greater contentment in this way. Nor do you have to be alone. You can effectively use this method of meditation whenever and wherever you are so moved.

These techniques for centering myself have played a key role in my practice of contentment. While I have never experienced the transcendental tranquility which many master mediators have written about, I *have* experienced many momentous moments of contentment by centering myself through the acts of consciously breathing, purposely praying, and regularly meditating.

Chapter 20

Do Your Best

"Always do your best.
What you plant now, you will harvest later."
Og Mandino[39]

Putting forth your best effort is integral to any and all of the actions involved in the practice of contentment. It's essential that you do your best to become aware of and accept the arrival of a not-enough thought so as to neutralize its discontent-evoking energy. It's equally essential that you do your best to re-parent yourself, unwind yourself from worry, remind yourself of the whys and wherefores of not-enough thinking, and center yourself in your sweet spots.

Always doing your best to practice contentment requires persistence and patience. Having been so thoroughly conditioned to believe that contentment can derive from the pursuit of more, better and/or different things, doing your best to break free from this habitual way of thinking requires the diligence and determination primary

[39] A 20th Century American author who wrote the bestselling book, *The Greatest Salesman in the World*, which sold fifty million copies and has been translated into over twenty-five different languages.

to persistence. It also requires patience as you strive to do your best to accept the seemingly endless occurrences of unappreciative thoughts so as to activate new and enhance the efficacy of your existing sweet spots.

With persistence and patience your perspective about the occurrence of not-enough thinking will change. You will come to perceive each occurrence as *grist for the mill*. Like a mechanical mill changes grain into flour, you will perceive each occurrence of a not-enough thought as grist for your mental mill, transforming the inner energy generated by this type of thinking into a force for contentment instead of discontentment. You will no longer look upon the arrival of an unappreciative more, better, different thought as something bothersome, burdensome or bad but, rather, as another opportunity to appreciate who you are and what you have. You will come to appreciate this as a chance to strengthen the energy of your sweet spots to generate greater extents of the satisfaction and serenity constituent of contentment. To paraphrase Og Mandino, you will realize that with the persistent and patient practice of contentment you will continually "plant now" seeds of appreciative thoughts from which you can "harvest later" the natural wealth of contentment.

Sometimes, however, our circumstances may make it difficult or even nearly impossible to "always" do our best to practice contentment. Even the most practiced can become complacent, forgetful and lazy from time to time. Similarly, we may become so steeped in stress and struggle that doing our best might only consist of counting to ten, biting our tongue, or taking some other sort of action that won't add to the efficacy of our sweet spots to generate contentment but will at least prevent us from devolving into deeper depths of discontentment. At other times, we may be experiencing such extreme emotional and/or physical pain that the illumination provided by our awareness is so dim and our capacity to accept a not-enough thought is so slight that it's virtually impossible to infuse our sweet spots with appreciative thoughts much less activate new ones.

These are the kinds of circumstances in which it is especially important to recall that the practice of contentment is about progress not perfection. Doing our best in this practice is very different than being perfect at it. You can steadfastly strive to do your best at anything, including the practice of contentment, yet it's undeniably unrealistic to believe that perfection is possible. Indeed, trying to be perfect is a set up for failure. In regards to the practice of contentment, expecting perfection at all times is not only unrealistic but sure to prolong our presently prevailing mood of discontent.

Reflections

Before I embraced the practice of contentment, I perceived that doing my best involved taking whatever actions were necessary to acquire and achieve more, better, and different things: more and more accolades and accumulations, better and better lifestyles and luxuries, and different upon different clients and customers. I was first and foremost focused on what I didn't have with barely any appreciation for what I did have.

Now, I see doing my best as taking whatever actions are necessary to generate more, better, different moments of contentment. While there is still a focus on "more, better, different," it is now grounded in great appreciation for who I am and what I have already achieved and acquired.

As I mentioned before, there is nothing intrinsically wrong or bad about more, better, different thinking. The left side of the brain is hardwired and conditioned to think in more as opposed to less, better as contrasted with worse, and different versus same terms. It's the extent of our appreciation that determines whether this type of thinking will generate contentment rather than discontentment. The larger the supply of appreciative thoughts stored in our sweet spots, the greater we will experience the awesome sense of peacefulness which comes with contentment. Indeed, the more we are able to cultivate appreciation and thoughtful action, the more we experience the joyfulness concomitant to contentment.

Doing our best to appreciate who we are, what we have, and our accomplishments is the key to unlocking the natural wealth of contentment. When our more, better, different thoughts are largely based in appreciation, the energy they generate will add to our supply of sweet spots and spontaneously spawn greater and longer lasting moments of contentment. We will no longer subconsciously sabotage our innate capacity for contentment. It won't matter how many worldly goods we have accumulated or how many goals we have accomplished.

It is for all of these reasons that I do my best to practice contentment in all aspects of my everyday life. No matter what I'm doing or where I am, I strive to notice any degree of discontent I'm experiencing and then do my best to see it as grist for my mental mill. I strive to perceive it as another opportunity to add to the stockpile of the appreciative thoughts stored in my sweet spots so as to change its energy into a force for contentment instead of discontentment.

Nonetheless, there are times when it's still really difficult for me to always do my best to practice contentment. Sometimes, as is currently the case for me, it's very hard for me to view my decades-long and increasingly worsening intestinal pain as grist for my mental mill. Despite my best efforts, I periodically fall prey to unappreciative more, better, different thinking: *there should be "more" that can be done to alleviate my pain; I wish the treatments and surgeries I have endured had produced "better" results; there must be something "different" that will cure my condition.*

Gratefully, I know based on results that persistently and patiently doing my best to become aware of and accept each occurrence of not-enough thinking about my intestinal condition will add to the contentment-generating efficacy of the sweet spots which formed from my appreciation of the many other ways in which I am physically and psychologically healthy. I also know, in regards to my intestinal condition as well as any other difficult situation or circumstance I encounter, that the practice of contentment is aimed at progressing towards greater and longer lasting moments of contentment—not the unequivocally unrealistic goal of perfecting it. Thus, I continually put forth my best effort to always do my best to take those kinds of actions which will populate my mind with predominately appreciative thoughts and bring forth a prevailing mood of contentment instead of discontentment.

MOVING FORWARD

*"The most useful piece of learning
for the uses of life is to unlearn what is untrue."*
Antisthenes[40]

The quintessence of moving forward in the practice of contentment is to "unlearn what is untrue" about unappreciative more, better, different thinking. Specifically, a practitioner of contentment strives to appreciate that this type of delusional, fantastical and fictional thinking can never evoke the satisfaction and serenity constituent of contentment. As such, the "most useful piece of learning" in the practice of contentment is to become knowledgeable about and adept at several key concepts: (1) using your awareness to trace any discontent you experience back to the not-enough thought that preceded it; (2) accreting acceptance of your unappreciative thoughts by acknowledging, surrendering and forgiving their occurrence so as to form new and activate your existing sweet spots; and, (3) doing your best to take whatever actions will infuse your sweet spots with contentment-generating appreciative thoughts.

---

[40] An ancient Greek philosopher who was a disciple of Socrates and stressed the importance of living a virtuous life.

The practice of contentment is a life-long work-in-progress, not a one-and-done achievement. A practitioner of contentment moves forward by patiently and persistently becoming progressively aware and accepting of the occurrence of an endless stream of unappreciative more, better and different thoughts and subsequently taking actions which will predominately populate his mind with appreciative thoughts. Indeed, the process itself is the product of this enduring practice.

In addition to becoming increasingly appreciative of what you already possess and have accomplished, as a practitioner of contentment it's likely that the way you appear and present yourself to others will change as your practice of contentment evolves. Thus your family, friends, workplace colleagues and others with whom you connect are apt to notice your ability to respond rather than react to the vicissitudes of life, an ability cultivated from having successively sown seeds of appreciation in the sweet spots which formed from your steady practice of contentment.

Some of the individuals with whom you are connected may admire and even be attracted to the calmness and composure consistent with your burgeoning contentment. You may become a role model for some people, thus sparking their interest in the practice of contentment. Indeed, my hope is that increasingly greater numbers of individuals will realize that they have the innate capacity for contentment. Likewise, I hope that these individuals will take whatever steps work for them, whether those presented in this book or any others they deem effective, to convert their unappreciative more, better, different thoughts into catalysts of contentment instead of discontentment.

Throughout this book, I have done my best to explain the practice of contentment as I understand and have practiced it so far. However, I don't pretend to have mastered every aspect of it. So I leave you with an invitation to join with me and others in an ongoing process to further refine and move forward in this practice by blogging at www.practicecontentment.com.

APPRECIATIONS

I am so appreciative of the many people who inspired and supported the writing of this book. The very notion of unappreciative more, better, different thinking first occurred to me while reading, *You Are That!*, a book by Gangaji, a contemporary American-born spiritual teacher and author. Since then my progression in contextualizing the material in this book and practicing contentment were greatly enhanced by the wisdom imparted by many other teachers and authors including, mentioning just a few, Eckhart Tolle, Jack Kornfield, the 14th Dalai Lama and his disciple in Phoenix, Arizona, ZaChoeje Rinpoche.

I am also so very appreciative of the various ways in which my wife, Jocelyn, caringly supported my writing of this book. She truly was the wind beneath my wings each time I faltered or wanted to give up on it.

I also want to express my appreciation for the continuous encouragement I received from the guys in the men's group of which I have been a member for over twenty years, namely, Barry Brooks, Jonathan Brooks, Ingolf Hermann, Douglas Jardine, and Arthur Weiss. Each of them in their own way supported my vision of making the material in this book as helpful as possible to others in dispelling their discontent.

Last but certainly not least, I truly appreciate the contributions made by Jennifer L. Weinberg, MD,

MPH, MBE to furthering a clear and concise presentation of the material in this book. Her edits and comments were consistently perceptive and productive.

49621559R10096

Made in the USA
Charleston, SC
29 November 2015